A Consen... ...ok
Co-opera... ...for
activists, ...co-ops and communities

by Seeds *for* Change

Published in 2013 by:
Seeds for Change Lancaster Co-operative Ltd
www.seedsforchange.org.uk

Illustrated by:
Carrie MacKinnon

Printed on recycled paper by:
Footprint Workers' Co-op
www.footprinters.co.uk

First edition, ISBN 978-0-9575871-0-6

THIS WORK IS
@NTI-COPYRIGHT.
FEEL FREE TO COPY,
ADAPT AND DISTRIBUTE IT
AS LONG AS THE FINAL
WORK REMAINS
@NTI-COPYRIGHT.

Contents

Foreword

This book is all about consensus decision making. In chapters one to six we look at the fundamentals of consensus decision making: what it is, how to do it, what qualities we need in ourselves and in our groups to make it work; along with tools and techniques to help when facilitating a consensus process.

The next two chapters are all about confronting the challenges we face in using consensus. Here you'll find troubleshooting tips, as well as an exploration of how to address deeper issues, such as interpersonal conflict and power dynamics.

The final chapter, *Consensus in wider society*, is different from the rest of book. In every other chapter we've aimed to share what we've observed and learnt as facilitators over the years, but in this chapter, which is about how a society based on consensus might work, we've allowed ourselves to dream a little. As well as applying our own experiences and observations we've included a lot of material based on intuition and guesswork. We find that the more we think about this subject, the more questions we have, and we hope that this chapter will create more questions in our readers, and hopefully some answers too.

In this book you'll find some words have been <u>underlined</u>. These refer to facilitation tools and techniques, and an explanation of them can be found in Chapter 6: *Facilitation techniques and activities*.

About Seeds for Change

Seeds for Change has been providing support and workshops to grassroots activists on consensus, facilitation and campaign skills since 2000. We've distilled our collective knowledge and experience into these pages, using new material along with extracts from resources created over the last eight years.

We're a network, currently made up of two workers' co-ops: *Seeds for Change Lancaster* and *Seeds for Change Oxford*, and all members are active in grassroots social and environmental justice campaigning as well as in the co-operative movement. We've been campaigning on various issues such as peace, roads, GM, climate change and have been involved in setting up and running various community resource centres. As the *Seeds for Change Network* we concentrate on working with grassroots environmental and social justice activists to help increase their effectiveness in campaigning and bringing about lasting positive change. Providing training, resources and support to grassroots campaigners is still the main focus of our work, and this is financed by donations and working part time as trainers for NGOs, co-ops and charities.

Particular thanks go to Carrie MacKinnon for all the illustrations she has done for us over the years, including for this book. But we would also like to thank all the many people and groups who have thought about, written about and talked about consensus and facilitation. We believe that there are no new ideas in the world, just recycled ones. The choice of words that make up this handbook (and any mistakes) are all our own. But the concepts, the experiences and thoughts that underlie what we have written have come from all over the world. In that spirit we make our resources and materials @nti-copyright so that others too may benefit in the way we have. *We encourage you to adapt, pirate, scavenge, recycle, translate, criticise, rebuild and redistribute anything and everything in this book.* Enjoy!

Further resources

If you're looking for materials to distribute in your group then have a look at the resources available on our website. You'll find introductory and longer guides to all the themes in this book, along with other topics of interest to grassroots activists. As with this book, these guides can be downloaded for free, and are @nti-copyright, so you can change or translate them to fit your group's needs.

We've listed other resources that we have found useful on the inside back cover.

www.seedsforchange.org.uk

Chapter 1:
Making decisions
by consensus

Consensus decision-making is a creative and dynamic way of reaching agreement between all members of a group. Instead of simply voting for an item and having the majority of the group get their way, a consensus group is committed to finding solutions that everyone actively supports, or at least can live with. All decisions are made with the consent of everyone involved, and this ensures that all opinions, ideas and concerns are taken into account. Through listening closely to each other, the group aims to come up with proposals that work for everyone. Consensus is neither compromise nor unanimity – it aims to go further by weaving together everyone's best ideas and key concerns – a process that often results in surprising and creative solutions, inspiring both the individual and the group as a whole.

At the heart of consensus is a respectful dialogue between equals. It's about how to work *with* each other rather than *for* or *against* each other – it rejects side-taking, point scoring and strategic manoeuvring. Consensus is looking for 'win-win' solutions that are acceptable to all, with the direct benefit that everyone agrees with the final decision, resulting in a greater commitment to actually turning it into reality.

Consensus can work in all types of settings – small voluntary groups, local communities, businesses, theoretically even whole nations and territories. The processes may differ depending on the size of the group and other factors, but the basic principle of co-operation between equals remains the same.

What's wrong with the democracy we've got?

How we make decisions is the key to how our society is organised. It influences every aspect of our lives including our places of work, local communities, health services, and even whether we live in war or in peace.

Many of us have been brought up to believe that the western-style system of voting is the highest form of democracy. Yet in the very nations which shout loudest about the virtues of democracy, many people don't even bother to vote any more; they feel it doesn't actually make any difference to their lives as most decisions are made by elite of powerful politicians and business people.

Representative democracies

Power and decision-making is taken away from ordinary people when they vote for leaders – handing over their power to make decisions to a small elite with very different interests from their own. Being allowed to vote 20 times in a lifetime for an MP or other political representatives is a poor substitute for having the power ourselves to make the decisions that affect every aspect of our lives.

Most social systems, including representative democracies rely on a system of hierarchy, where most of the power lies with a small group of decision-makers on top, while the much larger group of people at the bottom have little or no say. Those at the top would have you believe that such a system of hierarchy is the natural order of things. They argue that people are selfish by nature and need a set of morals, rules and laws to control behaviour. These rules need to be enforced by a system of control, where some people have more power than others. Leaders are necessary to tell people how to live their lives, direct them at work and structure society. They are backed up by police and military who use real or threatened violence to keep everyone within their law.

In addition, there are many areas of society where democratic principles have little influence. Most institutions and work places are entirely hierarchical – students and employees don't usually get a chance to vote their superiors into office or have any decision-making power in the places where they spend the greatest part of their lives. Or consider the supermarket chain muscling its way into a town against the will of local people. Most areas of society are ruled by power, status and money, not through democracy.

The alternatives are already here

The alternatives to the current system are already here, growing in the gaps between the paving stones of state authority and corporate control. We only need to learn to recognise them for the seedlings of the different kind of society that they are. Homeless people occupying empty houses and turning them into collective homes, workers buying out the businesses they work for and running them on equitable terms, gardening groups growing vegetables collectively. Once we start looking there are hundreds of examples of co-operative organising that we encounter in our daily lives.

Many of these people struggling for social change have recognised that changing the way we make decisions is key to creating a different society. It is by making decisions for ourselves that we exert control over our lives, and taste freedom. And since most of us wish to live in, and are dependent on, some form of society we must find ways to balance the needs and desires of every individual with those of the closer community and the wider world. We need a way of making decisions in which power is shared by all rather than concentrated in the hands of a few so we can all play an equal role in forging a common future.

A Consensus Handbook

What's wrong with voting?

Many people accept the idea that voting is the 'normal' way of achieving any kind of shared power over our future – after all, it is often presented to us as the only possibility out there. Compared to electing representatives, having a direct vote on important issues is clearly a significant step towards real democratic control. However, when you vote, any idea which most people like will be accepted, and the concerns of the people who opposed it can be ignored. This creates a situation in which there are winners and losers. This may foster bad feeling and distrust as the 'losers' feel disempowered by the process. The will of the majority may be seen as the will of the whole group, with the minority expected to accept and carry out the decision, even if it is against their deeply held convictions and most basic needs. It is possible for a voting group to look for solutions that would suit everybody, but it is more common for ideas with a majority backing to be pushed through. People might sometimes choose to go along with what the majority wants, but, in a voting system this is the only option. For example, if a group is trying to decide when to hold their regular meeting, a vote for the most popular time could exclude some people from the group altogether. If a group was applying for a grant, and a few people had a fundamental ethical objection to a particular funder, the group could press ahead regardless, even if it meant some people would feel forced to leave.

It's true that majority voting can enable even controversial decisions to be taken in a minimum amount of time, but that doesn't mean the decision will be a wise one, or even morally acceptable. After all, at one time, the majority of Europeans and North Americans supported the 'right' to hold slaves.

Why use consensus?

Looking for solutions acceptable to everyone who is affected is a much more co-operative model of decision making. The values of respect and equality that many of us try to apply with partners, family and friends are essential parts of consensus. If we were going out for a meal out with a bunch of mates we would try to find a place where everyone wanted to eat. The fact that a majority wanted pizza wouldn't be good enough if the coeliac and the vegan had to sit miserably picking at a green salad while everyone else gorged themselves on a feast. In this situation we might not identify that we were using consensus decision making, but the fundamental principles are the same. Respect for each individual means we are looking for an outcome everyone can live with. This means everyone working together to find a solution that is good for the whole group. When we transfer these principles to more important decisions and larger groups we need to put more thought into how we have those conversations. However, the goal – working co-operatively to make sure everyone's needs are met – remains the same.

By definition, in consensus, anyone can block a proposal by not giving their consent. This is not an option to be used lightly, simply because you don't like an idea – it means stopping other people going ahead with something they want to do and that should only be done in extreme circumstances. However it provides a safety net: the group knows from the outset that minorities cannot just be ignored, but solutions will have to be found to deal with their concerns. The right to block decisions is about much more than individual empowerment: it requires people to work together to meet both the individual's and the group's needs. This involves sharing power and responsibility, laying the foundations for a fairer world.

Who uses consensus?

Consensus is not a new idea. Variations of consensus have been tested and proven around the world and through time.

On the American continent non-hierarchical societies have existed for hundreds of years. Before 1600, five nations – the Cayuga, Mohawk, Oneida, Onondaga, and Seneca – formed the **Haudenosaunee Confederation**, which works on a consensual basis and is still in existence today.

There are also many examples of successful and stable utopian communes using consensus decision-making such as the Christian **Herrnhuter** settlement 1741-1760 and the production commune **Boimondeau** 1941-1972.

Christiania, an autonomous district in Copenhagen has been self-governed by its inhabitants since 1971.

Within the **co-operative movement** many housing co-ops and social enterprises use consensus successfully: prominent examples include Suma, a major UK wholefood wholesaler; and Radical Routes, a network of housing co-ops, social centres and workers' co-ops in Britain.

The business meetings of the Religious **Society of Friends (Quakers)** use consensus to integrate the insights of each individual, arriving at the best possible approximation of the Truth.

Political and social activists such as **anarchists** and others working for peace, the environment and social justice commonly regard consensus to be essential to their work. They believe that the methods for achieving change need to match their goals and visions of a free, nonviolent, egalitarian society. In protests around the world many **mass actions** and **protest camps** involving several thousand people have been organised and carried out using consensus, including the 1999 'Battle of Seattle' World Trade Organisation protest, the 2005 G8 summit protests in Scotland and the Camps for Climate Action in the UK, Germany, Australia, Netherlands and other countries. In 2011-12 consensus was used in almost every one of the hundreds of camps of the Occupy movement.

How does consensus work?

Conditions for consensus

Different groups use slightly different processes to achieve consensus decisions. However, in every group, there are a few conditions that underpin consensus building. The conditions also provide a useful set of pointers to possible underlying problems if your group is finding consensus difficult. See Chapter 8: *Bridging the gap between theory and practice* for more on how you might address these underlying problems.

Common goal: *everyone present needs to share a common goal and be willing to work together towards it.* This could be the desire to take action at a specific event, or a shared vision of a better world. In a longer term community it might be simply the desire to provide everybody with a home that is safe, comfortable and where all are equal. Don't just assume everyone is pulling in the same direction – spend some time together defining the goals of your group and the way you can get there. When differences arise in later meetings, revisiting the common goal can help to focus and unite the group.

Commitment to reaching consensus: *consensus can require a lot of commitment and patience to make it work.* Everyone needs to be willing to really give it a go. This means not only being deeply honest about what it is you want or don't want but also being able to properly listen to what others have to say. Everyone must be prepared to shift their positions, to be open to alternative solutions and able to reassess what they consider to be their needs. It would be easy to call for a vote at the first sign of difficulty, but in the consensus model, differences help to build a stronger and more creative final decision. Difficulties can arise if individuals secretly want to return to majority voting, just waiting for the chance to say: "I told you it wouldn't work."

Trust and openness: *we all need to be able to trust that everyone shares our commitment to creating true consensus decisions.* This includes being able to trust people not to abuse the process to manipulate the outcome of the discussion. If we feel scared that other people are putting their own wishes and needs before

everyone else's, then we are more likely to become defensive, and behave in the same way ourselves, because it seems like the only way to look after our own interests.

Making decisions by consensus is based on openness – this means learning to openly express both our desires (what we'd like to see happening), and our needs (what we have to see happen in order to be able to support a decision). Differentiating between what we want and what we really need sounds easy, but it can take time for us to learn how. If we are trying to win an argument, then an effective tactic is to claim we need more than we really do so we can concede points without giving up anything important. However, consensus is not about using tactics to try and win. It is about being honest from the outset so the group has the information it requires to take everyone's positions into account.

The consensus process

The key for a group working towards consensus is for all members of the group to express their needs and viewpoints clearly, recognise their common ground and find solutions to any areas of disagreement.

The diagram below shows how a discussion evolves during the consensus process. In the first stage the discussion opens out as people bring their perspectives and ideas to the group. This provides the material needed for a broad ranging exploration of all the options (the middle section) and helps people understand each others' concerns. This can be a turbulent and sometimes difficult stage – people might be grappling with lots of competing or contradictory ideas – but it's the most creative part, so don't lose heart!

Finally the group finds common ground and weeds out some of the options, combining all useful bits into a proposal. The third stage in the diagram below shows this drawing together of the discussion, culminating in a *synthesised* decision – one which brings together different ideas to meet different people's needs and concerns.

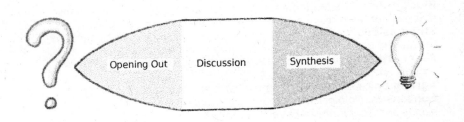

Opening Out   Discussion   Synthesis

The consensus process

Step 1: **Introduce and clarify the issue(s) to be decided**
Share relevant info. What are the key questions?

▼

Step 2: **Explore the issue and look for ideas**
1. Gather initial thoughts and reactions. What are the **issues** and people's **concerns**?
2. Collect **ideas** for solving the problem – write them down.
3. Have a **broad ranging discussion** and debate the ideas. What are the pros and cons?
Start thinking about solutions to people's concerns. Eliminate some ideas, shortlist others.

▼

Step 3: **Look for emerging proposals**
► Look for a proposal that weaves together the best elements of the ideas discussed. Look for solutions that address people's key concerns.

▼

Step 4: **Discuss, clarify and amend your proposal**
Ensure that any remaining concerns are heard and that everyone has a chance to contribute.
Look for **amendments** that make the proposal even more acceptable to the group.

▼

Step 5: **Test for agreement**
Do you have agreement? Check for the following:
Blocks: There is a fundamental problem with the core of the proposal that has not been resolved. We need to look for a new proposal.
Stand asides: I can't support this proposal because ... But I don't want to stop the group, so I'll let the decision happen without me.
Reservations: I have some reservations but am willing to let the proposal pass.
Agreement: I support the proposal and am willing to implement it.
Consensus: *No blocks, not too many stand asides or reservations? Active agreement?*

Then we have a decision!

▼

Step 6: **Implement the decision**
Who, when, how? Action point the tasks and set deadlines.

There are lots of consensus models out there, some groups have developed very detailed procedures, other groups follow a more organic process. The following basic process outlines the stages that are common to most models of consensus. It looks like quite a formal way of holding a discussion, but most experienced groups will go through these steps without noticing they are doing it.

If you have complex or difficult decisions to make, or if you are new to consensus, this process might help guide you through. Alternatively, if you are working more informally, but experience problems reaching a good decision, it's worth checking this process to make sure you have covered all the stages.

This model will work well in groups of about 2-20 people. With larger groups than that extra steps may need to be built in to ensure that everyone is able to participate fully. Have a look at Chapter 3: *Facilitating consensus in large groups* to see how this basic model can be adapted to work for groups of up to thousands of people.

The process in more detail

Step 1: Introduce and clarify the issue

This first stage is crucial to get you off to a good start. A good introduction will focus the meeting, ensure that everyone is talking about the same issue and provide everyone with all relevant information needed to make a decision. Spending a bit more time now to get everyone up to speed will save lots of time later and make it possible for everyone to contribute.

a) Explain the issue, and why it needs to be discussed.

This could be done by the facilitator, the person who is raising the issue or by someone who knows a lot about the issue and its background. Be careful to introduce the issue in a way that leaves options open. For example, if you start the discussion with: "Shall we get the builders in to fix the roof?" it implies far fewer possibilities than are opened up by: "The roof has been leaking, what shall we do?" (which might include sorting it out yourselves, or taking the opportunity to install solar panels at the same time, for example).

b) Share all relevant information.

If possible prepare a summary of the relevant information and circulate it in advance so that people have a chance to read up and think about the issue.

c) Agree the aims of the discussion

What decisions need to be made, and by when? Who needs to be involved in making the decision? What are the key questions? Can you break complex issues into smaller chunks to tackle one by one? Do all the decisions need to be made today? Could you decide the basics and leave the fine details to be worked out by a couple of people?

This is a lot to think about, and not all of these questions will be relevant every time, but they can help to narrow down and structure your discussion. For example, imagine you start with a vague heading on the agenda like "End of lease on building." Everyone will have a different idea what the discussion is about, and you may end up in a protracted wrangle about the pros and cons of other buildings before you have enough information to make a decision about them, or before you've even decided whether you want, or need to, move from where you are. By contrast, you could have a much more focused discussion opening with: "We have six months til the lease is up for renewal. Someone suggested we took the opportunity to find a different building. This is an important question that we all need to think about. The decision we need to make now is whether we are all totally happy staying here, or whether we want to look into other options. If we do decide to consider more options I suggest that we pass it on to a sub-group to investigate what they might be, and discuss it further when they report back."

d) Allow plenty of time for questions and clarifications.

Don't assume that everything is crystal clear, just because it's obvious to you. Equally, if you are confused yourself, now is the time to ask for more information or explanations.

A Consensus Handbook

Step 2: Explore the issue and look for ideas

Now it's time for everyone to really try to understand the issue, to express what they want or need to happen and to come up with lots of ideas for solving the problems.

a) Gather initial thoughts and reactions

Start by giving people space to think about the issue and to express any wishes and concerns that it brings up. Make a note of these as they will need to be addressed for a solution to be found. Resist the temptation to jump straight in with a proposal – to achieve consensus we first of all need to have a good understanding of everyone's concerns and limitations. Be honest about your own feelings and listen carefully to what everyone else is saying. At times it can be difficult to say what it is you want and don't want – if you're struggling to express things say so rather than staying quiet. Equally, if you don't quite understand someone else's position, ask for clarification.

b) Collect ideas for solving the problem

Use techniques such as <u>go-rounds</u>, <u>ideastorms</u> or breaking into <u>small groups</u> to generate lots of ideas for solving the problem.

Be clear that at this stage they are only ideas, not proposals. In consensus the word 'proposal' implies that you have thought carefully and are suggesting a way forward you think would be acceptable to everybody. It is too early to use this word before you know what people's thoughts and feelings are. When bringing up ideas take into account the concerns you've heard, and any objectives you've agreed. For example, maybe you are planning an action to protest against an army recruitment stall at your university careers fair. If you have agreed that you want to shut the stall down entirely, then holding banners in a different part of the university campus is unlikely to achieve your aim. If someone didn't want to do a noise demo because it might disrupt other stalls at the careers fair, they probably won't be happy with your suggestion to set the fire alarms off in the entire building. If you disagree with someone about what the aim should be, or you don't share their concerns, then open a discussion about it, don't just ignore what they've said and hope they'll forget. But if you accept what has been said, then show you have been listening by considering it when coming up with new ideas.

c) Have a broad ranging discussion about the ideas

Consensus is a creative thinking process that thrives on mixing up lots of different ideas. Make time for a broad ranging discussion, where you can explore ideas and look at the pros and cons and any concerns they bring up. This will often spark new and surprising ideas. Express any reservations about ideas early on so that they can be dealt with. Draw on all the experience, knowledge and wisdom in your group. Make sure everyone is heard.

Step 3: Look for an emerging proposal

After discussing the issue freely move on to finding agreement on what needs to be done.

This stage is also called *synthesis*, which means coming up with a proposal by combining elements from several different ideas.

Start with a summary of where you think the group is at. Outline the emerging common ground as well as the unresolved differences: "It seems like we've almost reached agreement on that part, but we need to explore this bit further to address everyone's concerns." It's important to not only pick up on clear differences, but also on more subtle agreement or disagreement.

Now start building a proposal from whatever agreement there is. Look for ideas on how the differences can be resolved. Focus on solutions that address the fundamental needs and key concerns that people within the group have. Often people are willing to give way on some things but not on others which affect them more closely. The solution will often be found by combining elements from different ideas. This might also mean digging a little deeper to find out why people want the things that they do. For example, maybe you are a housing co-op wanting to use your own home as a venue for an event, and one person is very resistant to the idea. Closer discussion might reveal you don't need to reject the idea outright – in fact their concern is about wanting to have privacy upstairs and in the kitchen, and if you only open up one room to the public and carry through an urn to provide tea they will be happy.

It can really help to use a flipchart or whiteboard to write up the areas of agreement and issues to be resolved. This means everyone can see what's happening and it focusses the discussion.

People often argue over small details and overlook the fact that they agree on the big picture. Making this obvious to the group can help to provide ways forward.

Even when there is strong disagreement within the group, synthesis can help move the discussion on. Always try and find some common ground, no matter how small: "So we're all agreed that climate change demands urgent action, even if we disagree on whether the solution lies in developing new technologies, or reducing consumption." This can reinforce that we're all on the same side, and remind a group of their overall shared aims – a necessary condition for consensus.

Synthesising a solution doesn't necessarily mean uniformity or unanimity. Sometimes a solution is staring us in the face, but our desire to get full agreement becomes an obstacle: "We're agreed we'd like to go ahead with a protest. However some feel strongly that the target of our protest should be government, and others feel it ought to be corporations – but do we have to choose between them? Could we not agree that both can happen?"

Step 4: Discuss, clarify and amend proposal

Check whether people have concerns about the proposal and look for amendments that make the proposal more acceptable to everyone. Do things like go-rounds and straw polls to gauge support for the proposal and to elicit amendments. If it becomes obvious at this stage that some people have strong reservations, see whether you can come up with a different, better option. Remember, consensus is about finding solutions that work for everyone. Be careful not to get carried away because most people like the proposal. Watch out for people who are quiet or looking unhappy and check with them. Give people time to get their head around the proposal and what it means for them. If it's a complex or emotional issue, it's good to build in some time for reflection or a break before moving on to testing for agreement.

Step 5: Test for agreement

a) **Clearly state the proposal:** it's best if people can see it written up, for example on a large piece of paper.

b) **Check for clarifications:** does everyone fully understand what is being proposed? Does everyone understand the same thing?

c) **Ask whether anyone has objections or reservations:** ideally the consensus decision-making process should identify and address concerns and reservations at an early stage. However, proposals do not always get whole hearted support from everyone, and less confident group members may find it hard to express their disagreement. It is important therefore to explicitly check if anyone is unhappy with a proposal at this stage.

Within consensus there are several ways of expressing disagreement: the block stops the proposal, while declaring reservations and standing aside provide a way to express concerns, but allow the group to proceed with the decision.

Exactly which of these are appropriate to use will depend on the situation and what the group has decided about how they want to use them.

A Consensus Handbook

Block: *There is a fundamental problem with the core of the proposal that cannot be resolved.* **If the group accepts the proposal either you or others will struggle to stay part of the group.** *We need to look for a new proposal.*

A block always stops a proposal from being agreed. It expresses a fundamental objection, not "I don't really like it" or "I liked the other idea better." The group can look for a completely different proposal, or look for amendments to overcome the objection. It is good to check for blocks first, because they can be harder to voice once a proposal has been given an enthusiastic go ahead by other people.

The block is a powerful tool and should be used with caution. Ideally strong concerns will be heard early enough in the discussion to feed into in the synthesised proposal and a block will be unnecessary.

Some groups place limits on the situations in which a block is allowed to be used – only when a proposal goes against the core aims of the group, for example. For other groups it is enough to say that it should only be used when feelings are so strong that the proposal going ahead would split the group. More on this can be found below, and also in Chapter 7: *Troubleshooting in your meeting.* However your group uses a block, it is important at this stage to remind everyone what the block means so everyone has the same understanding of how it should be used.

Stand aside: *I can't support this proposal because … But I don't want to stop the group, so I'll let the decision happen without me and I won't be part of implementing it.*

You might stand aside because you disagree with with the proposal: "I'm unhappy enough with this decision not to put any effort into making it a reality, but if the rest of you want to go ahead, I won't stop you." In this case the person standing aside is not responsible for the consequences. This should be recorded in the minutes.

Sometimes standing aside can be more pragmatic. You might like the decision but be unable to support it because of time restraints or personal energy levels. "I'm OK with the decision, but I'm not going to be around next week to make it happen." A stand aside on these grounds may not be relevant if a decision only takes a small number of people to implement it. For example, it wouldn't be necessary to stand aside from putting a banner up just because it was someone else who was going to attach it to the fence. However, if it is a decision about putting on an event, for example, which would take a lot of work, it is important to know if some people aren't around to help, and for them to formally step out of the decision making because it won't affect them.

The group may be happy to accept the stand aside and go ahead. Or the group might decide to work on a new proposal, especially where there are several stand asides. Again, this will depend on the situation. If group unity is very important then even one stand aside will be unacceptable. This might be because you are making a decision, such as about policy, which you need to trust everyone will implement, or simply that a major aim of what you are doing is to work together as a group. Supposing you planned a team-building social, and the proposal was to go rock-climbing. If one person stood aside because they were scared of heights and everyone else went ahead, you'd risk losing the whole point of the exercise.

Declare reservations: *I still have problems with the proposal, but I'll go along with it.*

You are willing to let the proposal pass but want to register concerns. You may even put energy into implementing the idea once your dissent has been acknowledged. If there are significant reservations the group may feel it necessary to amend or change the proposal.

Make sure that everyone understands the different options for expressing disagreement. Often people are confused and block when they would actually be happy to stand aside. Sometimes people are scared of blocking even though they are deeply unhappy and use a milder form of disagreement instead. Ask people what their problems with the proposal are, and whether they have suggestions for how they could be addressed.

d) Check for active agreement: if there are no blocks, and the group feels that reservations and standasides are within acceptable limits, check for active agreement from everyone. People often show they agree by waving their hands, but watch out for silence or inaction and check for the reasons.

A Consensus Handbook

Step 6: Implement the decision

Once you've agreed what you want to do you need to work out who will do what and by when. Share out the tasks among the group and record these action points in the minutes (see page 53) for the meeting.

Example of a consensus process

Step 1

"The bit of wasteland that we've used as a park for the last ten years is going to be sold by the council – they want to sell it so a supermarket can be built there!"

"But nobody wants another supermarket – we already have three in this town!"

"So, does anyone know when all this is likely to happen?"

[More information is shared.]

"So I guess the decision we need to make right now is whether we want to do anything about it, and if so, what."

Step 2

"Let's go round and see what everyone thinks."

"I guess it's time to find somewhere else for the kids to play."

"I don't think we should give up that easily – let's look for ways to raise money to buy the park!"

"Yeah, let's form an action group, do some fundraising, and what about squatting it?"

"Mmm... not sure about that. Not wanting a supermarket is one thing, but squatting the park's another – that's not for me! I'd be happy to look at how to raise the money, though."

"OK, but I don't want to rule out taking action if we can't raise the money – if we give in too easily the developers will snap up every bit of green space for miles."

[More ideas are talked about]

Step 3

"So what are we going to do? Some of you feel that we should build treehouses in the park to stop the developers, but we think we should try and raise money to buy the land."

"But nobody's said that they're actually against squatting the park – just not everyone wants to do that. And squatting might slow the council down so we have time to raise the money. Let's do both!"

"Yeah, and although I don't want to live up a tree – I don't want to be arrested – I'd be happy to bring food and stuff and work in the group that's doing fundraising."

Step 4

"So let's just check how everyone feels about that proposal. Let's do a go-round."

"I like the idea of both squatting and trying to raise the cash to save the park, but people have been talking about separate groups doing those. I feel that we really need to stay as one group – I think if we split they might try to play one group off against the other."

"I'm not sure about this – I don't want to put my kids in danger."

[Everyone has their say]

"OK, so there's a suggestion that we amend the proposal to make it clear that we stay as one group, even though we're both squatting and raising funds at the same time. And Hal has pointed out that for a while, the land will still be pretty much as it was before, so we can still bring our kids to the park just like now."

Step 5

"Right, we have a proposal that we squat the park to make sure that it doesn't get trashed, and at the same time we start doing grant applications to raise the money to buy the land to save the park for everyone. We're going to be very clear that we are one group doing both of these things, and we want to make sure it's safe for children to continue playing there. Does anyone disagree with this proposal?

A Consensus Handbook

Remember, the block stops the rest of the group from going ahead, so use it if you really couldn't stay in the group if we followed this plan. And you can stand aside if you don't want to take part in all or part of the plans. If you think we should consider any reservations you have then please let us know, even if you're still going to go along with it."

"Yes, I'm not sure we can raise that much cash, but I do think squatting it has good chances of getting results. I don't want to take part in the fundraising. I'm not going to stand in the way – so yeah, I'll stand aside from the fundraising bit."

"Yeah, I'm not sure about the fundraising either – I agree it hasn't got much chance. But I'll go along with it, because I reckon a lot of people here have experience of this kind of thing, so let's try it out."

"Does anyone else disagree? No? OK, I think we might have consensus. Let's just check – wave your hands if you agree with the proposal... Rob, just checking, because you didn't wave your hands – are you happy with the proposal? Ah, I see, yes... I hope your wrist gets better soon. Great, we have consensus, with one stand aside and one reservation!"

Step 6

"OK – so we're going to squat the land to prevent any trashing going on, and we need to start fundraising. We'll need to decide things like when we'll start squatting, what we'll need, whether we want to do a news release and tell the council. And for the fundraising we'll need to identify funds that may be able to help, and come up with ideas for raising some money through benefit gigs and stuff. How about we start to work out the details for the squatting part right now, and then we meet again tomorrow to work out what to do about the fundraising? Great. And we'll need to let people who couldn't make it tonight know what we've decided and make sure they can get involved."

Key skills and values for consensus

When do I use the block?

At the decision stage of the consensus process people have several options – to agree with the proposal (with or without reservations); to stand aside from the proposal but let the others proceed; or to block the proposal.

The option to block a proposal is based on the principle that no decision should be made without the consent of every member of the group. It is a defining part of the consensus process. It means that a minority can't be ignored, but solutions will have to be found that deal with their concerns. If a proposal is blocked, it means that the group can't move forward until it comes up with a different proposal that addresses the concerns that led to the block.

Many groups go for years without anyone actually using the block. The fact that the option is there serves as a safety net – people have to listen to each other's concerns properly at the discussion stage because they know any one person can stop something going ahead if their concerns are ignored. If the block is used a lot in your group, it is often an indication that something is going wrong earlier in the decision making process – for example you may be rushing, and not really listening to people's concerns.

Alternatively, it may be that people are using the block lightly, simply because they are not keen on an idea. It helps to share ideas about how strong your opposition needs to be to warrant a block. One yardstick that is often offered is "There are such fundamental objections to this proposal that either I or others would have to leave if it went ahead". The point of this is to be honest with yourself about how important something is – not to use it as emotional blackmail ("I'll leave if you don't do what I want!"). Nor does this mean that a division of the group is always a bad thing. A block could be an indication of a deep-rooted incompatibility between different members of the group. Repeated blocking by the same

A Consensus Handbook

people or over the same issues can be a sign that it would be better for the group to split or someone to leave. However, the option to block means that no-one is forced into this position on the basis of one profound disagreement.

There are different ideas about the kinds of reasons for which someone can use the block. Some groups only allow the block when a proposal goes against the core aims of the group. For example, someone in a peace group might block a proposal to accept funding from a company with strong links to the arms trade because it went against what the group was set up for. However, if their concerns came from a relatively unrelated area of their ethics, they couldn't stop the others doing what they wanted. So, if the funder was not involved in weapons, but the tobacco industry, it would be less clear that they had grounds to block on the basis that the proposal went against group aims.

In other groups, it is also acceptable to block on the basis of strong, personal values or needs. In the example above, other groups would allow the block on the basis of a fundamental objection to the tobacco industry, even if this is only held by one person. These groups argue that a decision can only be called consensual if everyone in the group has the right to withhold their consent for any reason – not just reasons to do with group aims.

Which approach a group takes may depend on their ethics and philosophy. A group which wishes to place a strong emphasis on individuals putting the interests of the collective first might choose to reserve the option to block for proposals going against group aims. For other groups limitations on the block undermines the idea that decisions are taken only with everyone's consent. If people are only allowed to block for a narrow range of reasons, this takes away the option for them to say no to something which goes against something fundamentally important to them.

Often the decision about what kind of block to allow will also depend on circumstances. A group with fluctuating membership may find it hard to build the trust, openness and commitment which underpins consensus building. Without this, some individuals might be more likely to use the block to push their own agenda, without real care or concern for the impact this has on everyone else. In this situation, only allowing the block for proposals which go against core aims of the group could limit the potential for abuse of power.

Another factor is the impact a decision would have on the person blocking and whether standing aside is a real possibility. For example, if a co-op decides that they want a new person to join, then this affects every other member, no-one could stand-aside from the decision and not be involved in it at all, unless they left the group altogether. By contrast, if the decision was about a one-off event, then someone could not get involved in that particular thing, and still be part of the group. A similar question is about how major a role the group plays in someone's life. For example, if the group provides someone's home or workplace, like a co-op or protest site, decisions are likely to impact much more on individuals involved than a campaign group that meets once a month. Similarly, the personal upheaval involved in leaving a group if it takes decisions you cannot live with is likely to be less if the group is a smaller part of your life.

Whatever your group's approach, a big responsibility comes with the option to block. The block stops other people from doing something that they would like to do, therefore it is only appropriate to use it if major concerns about the proposal remain unresolved when it reaches decision stage. A person considering blocking needs to think carefully about whether they need to block or whether standing aside from the decision – letting the others in the group go ahead – would be enough. At the same time, a group needs to think very carefully before pushing any course of action that one person is powerfully opposed to, even if they are not blocking.

A Consensus Handbook

Active listening, summarising and synthesis

Active listening, summarising and synthesis are core skills for participating in consensus decision making. Finding solutions that work for everyone requires a good knowledge and understanding of what everyone wants. This sounds obvious, but after half an hour's rambling discussion, it is easy for people to get sidelined simply because no-one heard, or remembered, their points. Broadly speaking, active listening enables us to hear what others are saying, summaries help remind us of the key points in the discussion and check we have the same understanding, while synthesis is the skill that allows us to draw together different bits of different ideas to form one proposal that works for everyone. These skills are also important for facilitation, but we have included them here because it is so important that everyone in a meeting takes responsibility for really listening to each other and looking for ways forward.

1) Active listening

Active listening is a key skill for taking part in consensus meetings. When we actively listen we suspend our own thought processes and give the speaker our full attention. Normally our understanding of a conversation is coloured by our own interpretations, experience and point of view. However, when we actively listen we try to get away from this. We make a deliberate effort to understand another person's position and their underlying needs.

It is important when actively listening to make the mental space – don't think about what you want to say but focus on the speaker. Avoid signs of impatience such as looking at your watch but encourage the speaker with open body language and eye contact. Where appropriate short questions or comments can help the speaker formulate their thoughts and let them know that they are being listened to. This might mean asking follow on questions, like: "How do you feel about that?"

Alternatively, repeating short phrases can encourage someone to elaborate or clarify, e.g.:

"I think it'd be mad to ask him for help again, so we'll have to work it out for ourselves."

"You think it would be mad..?"

"Yeah, because..."

This technique is particularly useful if you think the speaker might feel challenged by a direct question (like "Why do you think it would be mad?") or you want to avoid steering the conversation in a particular direction.

Active listening helps meetings in several ways. It helps us to understand how the speaker feels about a subject or situation and the underlying emotions, concerns, and tensions. It allows us to focus on the core issues of a speaker's message. It enables us to hear what the speaker is actually trying to say to us, and not what we want to hear. It also shows the speaker that we are interested in what they have to say.

2) Summarising

Listening on its own is a great tool for diagnosing problems and hearing underlying issues. There's a follow on stage to active listening that can help a group move forwards: succinctly summarising what's been said. Summarising reassures speakers they are being heard, and it can also help to focus meetings. Examples include: summarising after a period of discussion to clarify where you think the meeting has got to; or summarising after someone has been speaking for a long time to ensure that everyone understood the essence of the point that has been made.

To summarise well, always wait until the speaker has finished. Offer the summary tentatively and allow people to correct you if you get it wrong. Use phrases such as: "You seem to feel that...", "What I hear you saying is.... is that right?" If we say something like: "So you feel that..." and the speaker doesn't agree 100% then the misrepresentation may offend them. Rephrasing what someone has said in a few, shorter sentences will show that we have understood the key points they wanted to make and is likely to be more useful than trying to parrot what they have said word for word.

Good facilitation should include frequent summaries of the discussion as it develops. This includes both content and people's positions, whether it's been said or communicated in other ways (e.g. through non-verbal cues such as body language, facial expressions or with an agreed set of hand signals). Summaries are a good way for the group to be more aware of what stage the discussion has reached, and it can also help people who are visually or hearing impaired, or simply forgetful.

Some people find it helpful to take notes or write up key issues on a flipchart as the discussion happens. This makes a succinct and accurate summary much easier.

3) Synthesis

Bringing together different ideas and trying to find a proposal that is agreeable to everyone is at the core of consensus. We call this process synthesis: it maps out the common ground, finds connections between seemingly competing ideas and weaves them together to form proposals. Because this skill is particularly useful at stage three of the consensus process, where you are looking for proposals, we have included a more detailed description of how to achieve it there (pg 20).

Guidelines for consensus

Consensus relies on everyone's active participation. Here are some tips for how you can help make it work.

★ If you don't understand something, don't be afraid to say so.

★ Be willing to work towards a solution that's best for everyone, not just what's best for you. Be flexible and willing to give something up to reach an agreement.

★ Help to create a respectful and trusting atmosphere. Nobody should be afraid to express their ideas and opinions. Remember that we all have different values, backgrounds and behaviour and we get upset by different things.

★ Explain your own position clearly. Be open and honest about the reasons for your view points. Express concerns early on in the process so that they can be taken into account in any proposals.

★ Listen actively to what people are trying to say. Make a deliberate effort to understand someone's position and their underlying needs, concerns and emotions. Give everyone space to finish and take time to consider their point of view.

★ Think before you speak, listen before you object. Self restraint is essential in consensus – sometimes the biggest obstacle to progress is an individual's attachment to one idea. If another proposal is good, don't complicate matters by opposing it just because it isn't your favourite idea! Ask yourself: "Does this idea work for the group, even if I don't like it the best?" or "Are all our ideas good enough? Does it matter which one we choose?"

★ Don't be afraid of voicing disagreement. Don't change your mind simply to avoid conflict and achieve harmony. When agreement seems to come quickly and easily, be suspicious. Explore the reasons and be sure that everyone accepts the solution for basically similar or complementary reasons. Easily reached consensus may cover up the fact that some people don't feel safe, or confident enough to express their disagreements.

A Consensus Handbook

Chapter 2:
Facilitating consensus

Have you ever sat through a meeting that has dragged on and on, with tempers running high, people talking over each other and no decisions being made? Or maybe one person dominates the whole meeting and makes all the decisions, leaving you to wonder why you bothered turning up? Most of us can manage sitting through such a meeting a couple of times, but then we start finding excuses not to go any more, or at least wish we didn't have to.

Unfortunately this pattern is very common in groups of all kinds. It leads to frustration, inefficiency and eventually loss of group members. However with the goodwill of the group it is quite easy to turn around the style of meetings and actually make them an enjoyable and inspiring experience for everyone.

This chapter explores the concept of facilitation and how it can help in creating successful and positive meetings. This includes a section on how facilitators can make adjustments for people with physical and sensory impairments as well as a section on minute taking. You can find some further tips and techniques for facilitating large meetings in the Chapter 3: *Facilitating consensus in large groups.*

The role of meetings in group work

Meetings are a necessary part of working in any group – they give us the chance to share information, to reach decisions and to get jobs done. But meetings have another important function, which is often forgotten about – **group maintenance** (see *box right*). A good meeting not only gets work done, but also involves, supports and empowers the participants, creating a high level of energy and enthusiasm. A sense of community and connection to fellow group members is the basis for successful group work and social change. Good facilitation will help you to achieve all of this.

> ## Was the meeting successful?
>
> **Tasks** – *What* got done? Did you get the necessary results? Were problems solved, and were the objectives of the group met?
>
> **Maintenance** – *How* did it get done? How did people feel and how will this affect morale and group cohesion? Did the meeting make good use of the pooled talents? Was it enjoyable?

What is facilitation?

Facilitation is about helping a group to have an efficient and inclusive meeting. It combines a series of roles and tasks. These are often embodied in one person – the facilitator – but we encourage groups to think in terms of shared facilitation, with everyone sharing the responsibility for ensuring a meeting is well run, productive and participative.

> ## What the dictionary says:
>
> **Facilitation** – Fa-sill-i-tay-shun
>
> noun. *making easy, the act of assisting or making easier the progress or improvement of something.*

Learn to facilitate

Facilitation is a vital role that needs to be filled at every meeting. In small groups this function may be shared or rotated informally while difficult meetings or meetings with a larger number of participants (more than 8 or 10 people) usually benefit from having a clearly designated facilitator. However, all members of any meeting should feel responsible for the progress of the meeting, and help the facilitator if necessary.

Facilitation tasks include:

✓ helping the group decide on a structure and process for the meeting and keeping to it;

✓ keeping the meeting focussed on one item at a time until decisions are reached;

✓ making it easy for everyone to participate – drawing out quiet people, or those with the most relevant expertise, and limiting those who tend to do a lot of the talking;

✓ clarifying and summarising points, testing for consensus and formalising decisions;

✓ helping the group deal with conflicts;

✓ keeping the meeting to time;

✓ ensuring that a written record is made of any action points and decisions agreed at the meeting.

To ensure that the group is using the most effective means of working through topics the facilitator might introduce facilitation techniques such as <u>ideastorming</u>, <u>go-rounds</u> or <u>small group discussions</u> (see Chapter 6: *Facilitation techniques and activities* for more information).

A facilitator's skills and qualities

Good listening skills including strategic questioning to be able to understand everyone's viewpoint properly.

Understanding of the aim of the meeting as well as long-term goals of the group.

Confidence that good solutions will be found and consensus can be achieved.

Neutrality on the issues discussed. Trust in the facilitator is dependent on them avoiding manipulating the meeting towards a particular outcome. If this becomes difficult, or you know in advance that you'll struggle to remain impartial try:

★ stepping out of role and letting someone else facilitate;

★ making it clear when you're expressing your own opinion and when you're intervening as the facilitator;

★ trusting that someone else will express your thoughts or feelings on the issue;

★ asking someone else, in advance, to ensure your own opinion is mentioned.

Clear thinking and observation – pay attention both to the content of the discussion and the process. How are people feeling? What is being said?

Respect for all participants and interest in what each individual has to offer.

Energy and attention for the job at hand.

Assertiveness – know when to intervene decisively and give some direction to the meeting.

Facilitating or chairing?

Superficially a facilitator fills a role similar to that of the traditional chairperson. There are however important differences:

✗ a facilitator never directs the group without its consent;

✗ at no time does the facilitator make decisions for the group or take on functions which are the responsibility of the group as a whole;

✓ a good facilitator stays neutral and helps the members of the meeting be aware that it is their business that's being conducted. The success of the meeting is the mutual responsibility of the whole group. The facilitator needs to be aware of this and always get the group's agreement before using facilitation techniques or activities.

Who should facilitate?

The role of facilitator can be learnt by everyone – use your own experience of meetings and observe other facilitators. Learn from mistakes, from bad meetings as well as good ones. If the role of facilitator is rotated amongst group members, people can develop these skills. It is well worth running some training, aside from normal meeting times, to practice facilitation skills. These skills are not only useful in group meetings but also in informal settings, at work and at home.

Be aware that people's behaviour in groups is influenced by individual needs and past positive and negative experiences in groups. Try to spot the effects of your own behaviour patterns and work on identifying your own and other people's needs. For more on this see Chapter 8: *Briding the gap*.

A Consensus Handbook

Co-facilitation roles at a meeting

Instead of just one facilitator you may have two or more **co-facilitators**. You can share out more facilitation tasks amongst the group and make the job of facilitating easier and less intimidating. It is important for co-facilitators to agree before the meeting exactly what the roles in the meeting are and when and why they may change roles.

Co-facilitators can take turns and support each other. This is useful if the facilitator needs to step out of their role to take part in the discussion, have a break or when back-up is needed in cases of tension, conflict or confusion. Four ears hear better than two, so co-facilitators are useful to check understanding of what is being said.

Taking hands: One of the co-facilitators can take on the job of keeping track of whose turn it is to speak next, and of giving appropriate time limits to speakers.

Vibes-watching: Someone not actively facilitating can pay more attention to the emotional atmosphere of the meeting and watch out for individual members being affected. In situations of conflict and distress the vibes-watcher will intervene, for example by taking on the role of an intermediary, by taking time out with someone to listen to their concerns or suggest breaks and tools to improve the atmosphere of the meeting. Good vibes-watchers are able to sense underlying feelings by listening carefully and being aware of body language.

The timekeeper draws attention to the agreed time frame for the meeting and keeps the group to it, negotiating extensions for particular agenda items, or for the meeting as a whole, if needed.

Minute takers play a vital role at meetings: they keep track of decisions, take minutes or notes, collect reports, and also draw attention to incomplete decisions – e.g.: who is going to contact so and so, and when? Minute takers can also provide a summary of the discussion if needed. See page 53 for a guide to minute taking.

A **door keeper** is useful in public meetings or when some people may be late. The door keeper welcomes newcomers or latecomers and brings them up to speed on the meeting – aims, what's been covered so far in the agenda, how decisions are being made, as well as the practical 'housekeeping' information such as tea and toilets. A door keeper can prevent the flow of a meeting being interrupted to recap every time someone enters the room.

In very large meetings it is advisable to have a **practical co-ordinator** responsible for the venue, equipment, refreshments and notices. The co-ordinator can also gather people together to start on time.

Facilitating consensus

The key to helping a group towards consensus is to help all members of the group *express their needs and viewpoints clearly, map out common ground* and *find solutions* to any areas of disagreement. Active listening, summarising and synthesis are three skills that help the facilitator with this.

Active listening: When we actively listen we suspend our own thought processes and give the speaker our full attention. We make a deliberate effort to understand someone's position and their underlying needs, concerns and emotions.

Summarising: A succinct and accurate summary of what's been said so far can be really helpful to move a group towards a decision. Outline the emerging common ground as well as the unresolved differences. Check with everyone that you've got it right.

Synthesis: Find the common ground, and any connections between seemingly competing ideas, and weave them together to form proposals. Focus on solutions that address the fundamental needs and key concerns within the group.

For more on this see Chapter 1: *Making decisions by consensus*, page 20.

A Consensus Handbook

Facilitating a meeting – beginning to end

This section gives an overview of the tasks a facilitator may need to undertake in a meeting. Whatever your group does, good meetings are vital to working together well. Every meeting is different. Not all the points mentioned may be appropriate – use your own judgement and innovation. Whilst it's important that these tasks happen, it doesn't have to be the facilitator that does them all! Draw on volunteers in the group to help with the facilitation. Make sure that the goals of the group and members' expectations of the facilitator are clear to everyone. This allows the appropriate use of tools and suggestions.

1) Preparing the meeting

1. Find a time that most people are able to make. Think about patterns of daily activity, such as parenting, work, dinner time.

2. Find a venue that is big enough to accommodate everyone comfortably. Ensure the venue is accessible – can someone in a wheelchair, or with hearing difficulties participate as easily as possible? Does the venue itself put some people off (pubs and venues with religious affiliations can have this effect)? Finally, have you put clear directions on your publicity? Chapter 8: *Bridging the gap* discusses the accessibility of venues, and other practical issues (page 157).

3. Check whether anyone in the group has any particular needs so that you can prepare your facilitation accordingly: even small changes in styles of facilitation and careful choice of exercises can help those with disabilities to take a full and active part in meetings. The most important step is to talk to anyone facing accessibility difficulties, ideally in advance. They're in the best position to advise on how the facilitator can include them. It can help to understand a person's attitude – one person may wish to take a full part in the group's meetings, whereas another person may not be at all bothered that they don't take their turn to write

up the notes on a flipchart. Knowing about their attitude will also help you to gauge whether and how to offer support – one person may appreciate frequent check-ins from the facilitator, but another may find them embarrassing or annoying! Being aware of this will help you prepare your exercises and timings.

4. Prepare an effective agenda (see *box on previous page*).

5. Ensure everyone is informed about time, place and content of the meeting. Send out pre-meeting materials if necessary. Don't just rely on email or social media sites, unless you know everyone has internet access and uses it regularly.

6. Consider physical arrangements such as temperature, air quality, ability to hear and see. Think about any special needs people might have and how tò cater for them. Arrange the seating in an inclusive way – some groups find circles are best because they allow everyone to see each other, while other groups prefer rows so that people can seat themselves according to how committed they feel to the group. In the case of rows, many groups find a V formation useful, like sergeant's stripes with the point away from the front.

7. Gather materials needed for the meeting, e.g. watch, pens, marker pens, flipcharts, written presentations and proposals.

8. Find a co-facilitator who can take over in an emergency, if the main facilitator tires or wants to participate more actively in the discussion.

A Consensus Handbook

The meeting agenda

A well structured agenda is vital for a good meeting. The facilitator can help the group draw up agendas that are focussed on the aims of the meeting and are realistic. Remember: if the meeting is only an hour long, there should only be an hour's worth of items on the agenda!

You can either draw up the agenda at the beginning of the meeting, or better still prepare a proposed agenda in advance. It's important that everyone gets a chance to have an input and that the agenda is agreed by everyone.

To create an agenda first agree the aims for the meeting and then collect agenda items from the group, preferably in advance. Estimate the time needed for each item. Think about priorities for this meeting – what could be tackled another time or in separate working groups? Think about effective tools for controversial topics. Deal with difficult items after the group has warmed up but before it is tired. Alternate short and long items. How should the meeting start and end? Plan in breaks, especially for meetings longer than 1½ hours. Plan in an evaluation of the meeting near the end so you can learn for next time.

Write up the proposed agenda where everyone can see it (on a whiteboard or flipchart, for example) or make copies to give to everyone. This will be helpful during the meeting as well as democratising the process of agenda formation.

Ask yourself what you can cut from the agenda, or trim down if anything runs over your proposed time. Have some suggestions up your sleeve.

Sample meeting agenda for
Stop Newton Bypass
Start 7.00pm
- ★ Introductions (10m)
- ★ Campaign summary (5m)
- ★ Report back from working groups: media, finance, research, stalls (20m)
- ★ Should we meet with the planners? Questions to ask (30m)

Break (20m)
- ★ End of year do – when and where (10m)
- ★ Organising more stalls/leafleting (30m)
- ★ Next meetings (5m)
- ★ Any other business (10m)
- ★ Evaluation (10m)

End 9.30pm

2) Getting a meeting off to a good start

Welcome everyone as they arrive and find out who they are. Some groups designate a welcomer or 'doorkeeper' for newcomers. That way everyone is greeted by a friendly face, knows where the toilets, refreshments and fire exits are, and can be brought up to speed with the meeting progress if they arrive late.

Introduce yourself and explain the role of the facilitator(s).

Have an **introductory activity.** What you do really depends on the group. It might be a formal icebreaker or a few minutes chat – whatever you do make sure you don't alienate anyone, especially newcomers to the meeting. If people don't know each other or there are newcomers to the group, get everyone to introduce themselves – really important for welcoming new people. Encourage people to share more than just their names. You could ask everyone to state in a couple of sentences why they are here, or to share an interesting skill they have (e.g. "I can compose poetry in Mongolian"). Or ask for their favourite colour, food etc. If there are too many people this could be done in smaller groups.

Make sure people know how the meeting works: explain the time frame, subject, aims of the meeting, process for making decisions, responsibilities of the facilitator and what you aim to do. Agree with the group what behaviour is acceptable or not acceptable in the meeting (e.g. one person speaks at a time, non-sexist and non-racist language, no dominating or threatening behaviour). This may be agreed for a series of meetings, or unique to a particular meeting. This group agreement can be useful to have on display to remind people of what was agreed.

Explain the proposed agenda, then ask for comments and make necessary changes. Be careful not to spend half the meeting discussing which item should go where – if necessary be firm. Allocate time for each item and set a realistic finishing time. Keep to this. If using consensus decision making make allowance for extra time to go deeper into the issue if necessary.

Ensure roles such as minute taker, timekeeper and vibes-watcher are covered.

A Consensus Handbook

3) During the meeting

Make sure **everyone can see the agenda** – display it on a large sheet of paper. Flipchart paper or the back of a roll of wallpaper are ideal for this. You can cross off points once they are dealt with as a visual reminder that the meeting is getting things done.

A common way of starting is to recap recent events or the last meeting.

Go through the agenda item by item. Keep the group focussed on one item at a time until a decision has been reached, even if that decision is to shelve it for some other time.

Use short items, fun items, announcements and breaks throughout the agenda to provide rest and relief from the more taxing items.

Make sure that decisions include **what, how, who, when** and **where.** Ensure any action points are noted down along with who will do them and any deadline. Encourage everyone to feel able to volunteer for tasks and roles. If the same people take on all the work it can lead to tension and informal hierarchies within the group. It can help if the more experienced members of the group offer to share skills and experience.

If new items come up in the discussion make sure they get noted down to be dealt with later. You could choose to use a <u>parking space</u> for this.

Invite and move forward discussion. Clarify proposals that are put forward. State and restate the position of the meeting as it appears to be emerging until agreement is reached.

Introduce tools such as <u>ideastorming</u> options, forming <u>small groups</u> for discussion, delegating to working groups, and <u>go-rounds</u>, to make the meeting more efficient and participatory. Some exercises may not be suitable for everyone – consider what role hearing, sight and mobility might play in activities.

Regulate the flow of discussion by calling on speakers in an appropriate order. Often this will be as they indicate they want to speak. Sometimes you may ask more vocal people to hold back from speaking in order to let others have their say.

Help everyone to participate: draw out quiet people, limit over-talking, don't let anyone dominate the discussion. Use tools such as <u>talking sticks</u> or breaking into <u>small groups</u> to equalise participation and to create a safe atmosphere for expressing opinions and feelings. Consider participants' ability to actively take part in quick moving discussions – e.g. it may not always be clear who is saying what; fast or excited speech may be more difficult to understand. Use suitable language and exercises so everyone can participate.

Check on the overall feeling of the group throughout the meeting: check energy levels, interest in the subject, whether the aims are being fulfilled, whether the structure is appropriate (large or small groups) and time.

Be positive: use affirmation and appreciation; comment on special contributions of members and accomplishments of the group. Be even-handed and don't just affirm a few individuals.

In tense or tiring situations try humour, affirmation, games, changing seats, silence, taking a break etc. Some groups might rebel at the suggestion of 'wasting time' on a game, but will welcome a stretch break or informal hilarity.

Challenge put-downs and discriminatory remarks.

A Consensus Handbook

4) Ending the meeting

Make sure the meeting finishes on time, or get everyone's agreement to continue.

Make sure **a time and place for the next meeting** has been agreed and that people leave their contact details if they want to be updated or receive minutes for the meeting. Do this before people start leaving.

Sum up, remind people of what they've committed to doing before the next meeting, and provide some satisfying closure to the meeting. Remember to thank everyone for turning up and contributing.

Check that someone has taken responsibility for **writing up and circulating the minutes** or notes in the next few days.

Evaluating your meetings can help to constantly improve them. It's a good idea to leave a few minutes at the end of every agenda and ask the group what went well and what needs to be improved. You could also get together afterwards with the other organisers to evaluate the meeting. Remember to celebrate what you have achieved!

It can be nice to follow the meeting with an **informal social activity** like sharing a meal or going to the pub or a café. Think about any special needs – not everyone drinks alcohol, you might have vegetarians or vegans in your group and so on, so try to choose an inclusive venue or activity.

Making meetings accessible for people with physical and sensory impairments

Visual impairment

Potential challenges for those with visual impairments include light levels, handouts, flipcharts and whiteboards, and keeping track of the discussion – particularly if <u>hand signals</u> are used. Pre-printed materials should be made available in a variety of formats including large print. Although handouts can be adapted or recorded, it's obviously impossible to prepare all content, for example things written up as part of an ideastorm.

In some situations personal support may be useful and the facilitator can help out by providing more detailed summaries. These could include interpretation of handsignals (and other body language) that people are using, e.g. "I see that most people are waving agreement to that point, but some of you aren't..."; "Some of you seem really enthusiastic about that proposal, but I see that others aren't looking too excited".

Announcing your name before speaking, and using names rather than pointing is helpful: "Jo, Ann and Saff – you all have your hands up to speak." This lets a visually impaired or blind person know who is about to speak.

A Consensus Handbook

Hearing impairment

Deaf and hard of hearing people often struggle with large or echoing spaces and background noise at venues (such as traffic, buzzing strip lighting or other groups talking in the same room). The person concerned will usually know how they can best participate in a spoken discussion – the following are all possibilities that are worth asking about:

★ Summarise regularly, providing an additional chance for the flow of the discussion to be understood.

★ Make sure everyone can see each other clearly (to allow lip reading and to make sure sound isn't impeded by other people's bodies).

★ Write up all points on a flipchart or whiteboard (these can be used as clues to provide context, allowing educated guesses at whatever hasn't been heard).

★ Make sure people (especially the facilitators) speak clearly, not too fast, and look towards the deaf or hard of hearing person.

★ People should take great care not to talk over each other – only one person should speak at a time. The facilitator should be strict about this.

★ Have enough spaces available so small groups can work in different rooms to avoid background noise from other groups.

★ Human support (e.g. note takers; speech to text operators) can sit with hearing impaired people to write, type or speak summaries.

★ If the hearing impaired person requires a Language Service Provider (e.g. a lip speaker or British Sign Language signer) contact the Action on Hearing Loss (RNID) Local Communications Services Office or local disability rights information centre well in advance.

★ Finally, technical solutions may be relevant – induction loops at venues are common, but don't always work too well, so do check them before the meeting.

Motor and mobility impairment

Some mobility impairment issues will require practical adjustment or support at the venue – these are covered in Chapter 8: *Bridging the gap*, page 157. A good start is to familiarise yourself with the venue – what's the access like (steps, handrails, ramp etc.); is there an adapted toilet? Summarise and publicise access information in advance of your event – this sends a clear signal that you are prepared to make adjustments and provide assistance, and helps disabled people assess whether they feel they can take part.

As a facilitator you may also need to consider difficulties in speaking, or using <u>hand</u> <u>signals</u>. Plan the group's movements and physical activities (e.g. <u>icebreakers</u>, <u>energisers</u>, <u>role plays</u> and breaking into <u>small groups</u>) in such a way that they are inclusive. Things to watch out for here are: enough time and space to move; providing alternative suitable activities and where people are going to be positioned during exercises: sitting on the floor can create barriers for people with mobility impairments and blind people – those unable to sit on the floor will be at higher levels and may feel isolated.

Top Tips for Facilitators

★ Design a good agenda. Be realistic about what the meeting can achieve. Set time limits and tackle all points.

★ Be aware of both content and process.

★ Keep the group moving towards its aims.

★ Use a variety of facilitation techniques to keep everyone interested.

★ Create a safe and empowering atmosphere to get the best contribution from everyone.

★ Put a stop to domineering behaviour, interrupting, put-downs and guilt trips.

Taking minutes

Minutes are a written account of the meeting, covering the main points of discussion, the decisions reached and actions to be taken. Keeping and *reading* minutes is helpful in several ways:

★ Minutes remind people of what they said they'd do and by when.

★ They provide an accurate record of decisions for the future when people's memories fail or when they disagree about what's been decided. This also helps avoid having to go over the same ground again and again.

★ They inform people who were absent from the meeting about what happened and what was decided. They also provide a way for new members of the group to get up to speed with the group's actions and decisions.

★ During the meeting the minute taker can support the facilitator by checking that the **what, who, where** and **how** are covered for each decision made. The minute taker can also help move the meeting along by providing a summary of the discussion on the basis of the notes they've taken.

Top tips for minute taking

★ Clearly mark decisions and action points so they are easy to spot.

★ If the minutes are long, provide a brief summary of key decisions and action points at the top of the minutes.

★ You could even sort the action points per person so everyone can see at a glance what they need to do.

How to write minutes

Traditionally minutes are a blow by blow account of the meeting, covering the major points that were made, the flow of the argument, and the decisions reached. However for most meetings a much shorter version is adequate, covering decisions made and action points to be carried out.

Check with everyone how detailed they want the minutes to be. Sometimes a more detailed account can help those absent from the meeting understand why particular decisions were made, avoiding having to explain everything in the next meeting.

At the beginning of each meeting go through the minutes from the previous one. Record any corrections or additions and ask for the group's approval.

Minutes usually include the following:

★ name of the group;

★ date, time and place of the meeting;

★ list of people present and absent;

★ amendments or approval of the minutes from the previous meeting;

★ for each agenda item:

   ☆ summary of the issue and information shared;

   ☆ summary of the discussion, capturing key points, proposals and decisions, including action points (who, what, where, when);

★ next meeting – date, time, location, proposed agenda items;

★ name of person taking the minutes;

★ any attachments such as relevant reports, budgets etc.

Distributing minutes

Once you've written up the minutes, make sure they get distributed to everyone who needs a copy as soon as possible. Not only does this encourage a culture of getting things done, but also many people will wait until they see the minutes before they take action. If for some reason you are unable to send out the minutes on time, don't be afraid to ask for help.

Decide during the meeting how the minutes will be distributed. Who needs a copy? How widely do you want to circulate them? Will it be on paper, via email or on the group's website or wiki?

You also need to work out a way of storing them in the long-term that is safe and easily accessible – this could be a folder of paper copies or on a web-based archive.

Privacy and security

Minutes provide lots of details about your group and individual members. Some of this info may well be sensitive and should stay within the group (e.g. if you're a campaigning group you may not wish to reveal your plans to the developer you're fighting.) Corporations and the mainstream media have all been known to get hold of internal documents and use them to their advantage. As a group, work out how secure you need to be and what levels of privacy members expect. Agree how openly accessible the minutes will be: internally on paper only, on email-list or published on your group's website for all to see? What details really need to be written down?

An ABC of minute taking

Good minutes are:

Accurate. Record proposals and final decisions word for word and read them back to ensure accuracy. Separate fact from opinion. Facts are objective and indisputable; opinions are personal views.

Agreed. Avoid misrepresenting anyone's contribution by asking everyone to agree the minutes. If the minutes are going further afield than those present at the meeting, get agreement before circulating them.

Accessible. Use accessible language: avoid jargon, in jokes and personal shorthand. Is email OK for everyone? If not use post as well. Will everyone be able to open an electronic document in the format you usually use? Do you need large print copies for visually impaired participants?

Allocated. Make sure action points have *who* and *by when* next to them. If they lack either you may need to approach people and clarify the action point. If someone was volunteered to do a task in their absence, check with them before they read it in the minutes! If they can't do the action point, find someone who can.

Brief but informative.

Clear. Write the minutes so that someone who wasn't at the meeting would be able to understand them. That way they'll be clear and comprehensible.

Complete. Ensure any documents mentioned are either attached or referenced, so people can find them (e.g. provide links to a website).

Circulated. The job doesn't stop with typing them up!

A Consensus Handbook

Chapter 3:
Facilitating consensus in large groups

Trying to find consensus in a large group brings its own challenges and rewards. The conditions for good consensus still apply, but might be harder to achieve in a bigger, more diverse group. You should go through the same process you usually use to reach consensus, but remember each step may take longer and require some specialised facilitation tools. Consensus requires active participation from everyone – much harder to achieve in a large group of people. But when it's working, consensus in large groups can be exhilarating and inspiring!

Below you'll find lots of tips for making consensus work in large groups, including an outline of the spokescouncil which has been used successfully by groups of hundreds and thousands of people.

In this chapter we focus on how to make consensus decisions in large groups, but many of the tools we explain can be used not just for making decisions, but also to share information and ideas. Bear in mind that in any organisation or network decisions are usually easiest and best made by the people directly affected by them. Make sure that you're not dealing with questions in a large group that can and should be dealt with at a lower level.

A Consensus Handbook

Meeting the conditions for consensus in large groups

Consensus in large groups poses particular challenges. Large groups can:

★ make it more difficult for less assertive people to participate. Not everyone is comfortable speaking in front of a large meeting;

★ be easily dominated by a confident few;

★ have a slower pace and lower energy than smaller groups – taking longer to reach decisions.

Extra care needs to be taken to ensure that the conditions for consensus are met – group members must share a common goal, be willing to build trust and respect and be able to actively participate in a clear and well facilitated process. You may wish to have a look at the section on conditions for consensus in Chapter 1: *Making decisions by consensus*, page 12.

Common goal: whether it's a national campaigning network or a temporary group coming together for a mass protest, in any large group of people you need to be clear why and to what extent you are working together.

The Occupy movement, starting in 2011, generally made little attempt at finding common aims between those involved. It was accepted that there would be at least as many goals as there were individuals in the movement – something which inevitably make the common goal condition (and therefore consensus) impossible to achieve at times.

Often, and particularly in more traditional groups, a smaller founding group of people decide in advance what the overarching aims of the group will be and then invite people to participate on that basis. This way, you can still tweak the aims with the whole group later, but you'll all be starting from a similar place. Other groups and networks may start with a blank piece of paper and work on the aims together, which can take a lot of time and patience but enables full participation in the process.

Once agreed, **a written statement of the aims and workings of the group** serves as a reminder and can be used to bring new members up to speed – so that both the new members and the existing group are sure that everyone is working towards the same goals. Make sure you explain to new people what's already been decided and what is still open to discussion. It also helps to run introductory sessions, where new people can find out what the group is all about and decide whether it's the right group for them.

If you can't find enough common ground you may consider splitting into several groups, and continuing to work together as a network on the points you do agree on.

Coalitions and alliances formed between pre-existing groups, for example to fight a specific issue, can find it difficult to reach consensus. Often the groups involved have different aims and ways of working and some may not be committed to consensus, but are more interested in pushing their politics on everyone else. This can easily happen if one of the groups in a coalition is or has been involved in more mainstream ways of organising – lobbying before meetings is often seen as acceptable, but can make it difficult for people to actively listen to each other and to be honest about their own positions.

Don't forget that above all, consensus does not mean agreeing on everything or having unanimity. Whenever possible, encourage a wide range of different actions which work towards your agreed aims.

Trust is more difficult to achieve in large groups as it's harder to get to know one another. Spend time discussing aims, people's politics and motivations. Social time is important too. Build in ways for new people to get to know at least some of the people in the group quickly.

A clear decision making process will help people to trust that they will be heard and respected in the final decision.

Clear process: if you are going to work by consensus it's vital that you explain to everyone the basics of how it works. Take time at the beginning of each meeting to explain the agenda, how decisions are made and how to participate. Run regular workshops in consensus and facilitation. Use flip charts to write up the consensus flowchart, the agenda, key points of the discussion and key decisions and put them up around the room so that everyone can see them.

Large meetings need more preparation and planning. Often a tight structure will be useful, however this can also be overly restrictive. Try to strike a balance between structure and open flow. Work out which items need to be discussed and agreed by everyone and which can be delegated to smaller groups.

Time: allow extra time for large group meetings so that people feel that there's been adequate discussion and an opportunity for people to express and hear all ideas. Cutting off discussion and forcing a decision will leave lots of people feeling disempowered and frustrated.

Facilitation: you will need a facilitation team that is seen as impartial, and who know exactly what job they are doing – someone to facilitate, someone to take hands, someone to write up notes on a flip chart, maybe a separate timekeeper and a doorkeeper, someone to prepare refreshments.

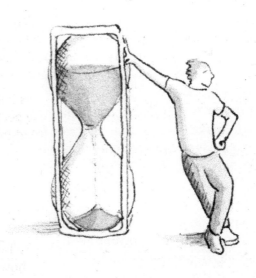

Processes for large groups

Decisions made in large groups can be inspiring – collectively coming to good decisions and seeing that everyone supports the agreement reached. However, to make this possible, thought needs to go into how to adapt the process to deal with challenges that larger groups throw up.

The six steps for reaching consensus are the same as for small groups, but some steps may happen with everyone together and other steps may happen in small groups to enable in-depth discussion and participation. Processes developed for large groups include delegation, large plenaries, splitting into small groups and the spokescouncil. Usually a combination of processes is needed for a smooth and successful large meeting.

Delegation and accountability

Some issues are important enough that everyone should be involved in the discussion and decision making. However, large groups of people have a tendency to micro-manage all work due to a lack of trust or imagination, leading to every single detail being worked out in the large group. But does it really need everyone to discuss the exact wording of the news release, or the order of bands for the benefit gig?

A good rule of thumb is that decisions should only involve those that are affected by it. Make decisions on policy or framework in the whole group and delegate the implementation and detail to working groups. Trust people to work in the spirit of the group and the agreements you've made together. This way you can save everyone lots of time and frustration.

Accountability is an important factor in building trust. It also makes it more difficult to accumulate power and avoids corruption – both are common pitfalls of organising on any scale. Build in regular report backs so that the whole group is kept informed about the work sub groups are doing and that they are both accurately representing their group and acting within their mandate.

A Consensus Handbook

Large plenaries

Large group plenaries, where the whole group comes together in one place, can be used to share information, to make proposals and for final decision-making.

However plenaries are much less useful for discussions that involve everyone. Large group discussions tend to be dominated by a few confident people – most people won't feel confident enough to speak in front of hundreds of people. There are also time constraints – giving everyone just three minutes to speak in a meeting of 200 people would take at least 10 hours! Plenaries are also limited by numbers – too large and people won't be able to hear and see each other or even fit into one room.

If you do hold a large plenary meeting then consider how to increase access and participation. You can limit the number of times a person can speak and give preference to those who haven't yet spoken. To help with clarity, summarise regularly and write up key words for everyone to see. Make sure everyone can hear each other. This might require some system of amplification or relaying.

Working in small groups

The advantages of splitting into small groups for discussion are that they create safer, more dynamic spaces to work in and include more people in the discussion. People will be much more comfortable talking openly in a small group of 6-15 people. Working in small groups also saves time, particularly if each group discusses a different element of the topic in parallel.

Working in small groups usually begins with the whole group starting to discuss the issue: sharing information, highlighting problems and drawing up a list of possible ideas. Then people split into small groups to discuss the ideas and come up with more. You can either ask each group to explore all the ideas, or each group could take away just one idea to examine it in depth. The small groups return to the main forum and report back, highlighting possible obstacles to each idea. If full group discussion cannot resolve the obstacles, small groups can go away to try to find ways to solve the problem. They report back, and this process continues until the obstacles are overcome, a proposal is formed, and a decision is made.

Some people resist small group work. It requires trust to let other people go away and discuss an issue, and that trust isn't always present. Some people just like having a larger audience, others struggle to choose between working groups. To reassure people and to make sure that ideas and points don't get lost, it's important to have a well-functioning feedback process. It is good to explain that feedback will happen, give groups guidelines on good feedback and to set aside some time for the small group to agree what to feed back to the large group.

This process is still limited by size as it involves some plenary discussions. The spokescouncil process below expands on the idea of breaking up into smaller groups to enable decision-making on a much larger scale.

The spokescouncil

The spokescouncil enables large numbers of people to work together democratically, permitting the maximum number of opinions and ideas to be heard in an efficient way. It allows consensus decisions with hundreds, even thousands of people (such as at the G8 Horizone camp in Scotland in 2005, anti-nuclear Castor mobilisations in Germany and various Camps for Climate Action). It is used successfully by many groups such as social centres, workers' co-ops, peace and environmental movements.

How it works

In a spokescouncil the meeting breaks up into smaller groups, which start by discussing the issue(s) to come up with concerns and ideas. If a small group can reach agreement on a preferred proposal, or develop some guidance on what would be acceptable to the group, that may speed up the process, but it isn't always possible.

Each group then sends their spoke (delegate) to the spokescouncil meeting, to present the breadth of ideas and concerns of their group, plus any proposals and ideas. The spokes together look for one or more proposals that they think might be acceptable to all groups and then take these back to their own groups for discussion and amendments.

Each small group checks whether there is agreement which is then reported back to the spokescouncil by the spokes to check whether there is agreement by all, or if not to draw up new proposals. The power to make decisions lies firmly with the small groups, not the spokes.

Roles within the spokescouncil

Small groups are often based around pre-existing groups such as work teams within a business or organisation, local groups within a national network or affinity groups on a mass action.

Alternatively, a large group might split into smaller groups just for the duration of one meeting, in which case groups can be created entirely randomly, or by grouping people around something they have in common such as a shared language or living in the same area.

The **spoke's** role is to feed back information between the small group and the council. The spoke needs to act as a voice for *everyone* within the small group, communicating the breadth of collective thought rather than their own personal point of view. Being the spoke carries a lot of responsibility to represent information accurately and not to manipulate the process.

Generally spokes do not make decisions for their group. They will always check back for agreement before a decision is finalised. However, an individual small group may choose to empower their spoke to take decisions within agreed parameters.

For a spokescouncil to work effectively and democratically, everyone needs to be clear about the role of the spoke, and how much power the group has given their spoke. It's very easy for a spoke, without even noticing, to represent their own view rather than the group's. Ideas can get lost or misrepresented in the transmission between small groups and the spokescouncil. Informal hierarchies may develop if it is always the same person acting as spoke.

To avoid these problems you could appoint two spokes, one to present viewpoints and proposals from their small group, the second taking notes of what other groups have to say. Spokes can be rotated from meeting to meeting, or agenda item to agenda item.

The facilitation team: good facilitation is key for a successful spokescouncil – it's a fairly complex process so you'll need a team of people to keep an overview and help small groups and spokes when they get stuck. As well as being accepted as impartial, the facilitators will need to be able to spot emerging agreements and potential sticking points. Being skilled at synthesising a large number of proposals and keeping the meeting focused are a definite bonus.

You'll need a team of at least four facilitators who work well together. One facilitator to facilitate the spokescouncil, one for writing up the discussion on flipcharts and looking for possible agreement. Another to watch out for the time, and the general mood of the meeting. Finally, you'll also need someone to take minutes.

Allow small groups enough time for discussion. If small groups struggle to come to an agreement within a reasonable time the spoke can feed back the whole breadth of opinion within the group.

In groups with international participants, or those who use sign language you might need to allow time for translation. Check in advance so that you can arrange for translators.

Case study: Spokescouncils in practice

Radical Routes is a UK wide mutual aid network of co-ops which uses the spokescouncil structure for their Business Meetings. These usually take place four times a year.

An agenda for each meeting is sent out beforehand so that member co-ops can discuss the agenda items, and tell their representative how to respond to proposals in the meeting. Representatives may have a remit of what's OK to agree to, and when they have to go back to their co-op for instruction.

If a new proposal comes up or a proposal is changed during the course of the meeting, people may feel that their co-op will be OK with it, or that they should check back with their co-op. If there are any changes to the proposal, even if agreed by the reps, it does not become policy until it is ratified at the next meeting, giving a chance for everybody in each member co-op to be aware of and agree to the changes.

The stages of the consensus process for large groups

| Discussions in the spokescouncil | Feedback through the spokes | Discussions and decisions in small groups |

Step 1: Introduce and clarify the issue(s) to be decided

Share relevant information. Work out what the key questions are. This step can either happen with the whole group together or just with the spokes in the spokescouncil who then feed back to small groups.

▼

Step 2: Explore the issue and look for ideas

1. Gather initial thoughts and reactions. What are the **issues** and **concerns**?

2. Collect **ideas** for solving the problem – write them down.

3. Have a **broad ranging discussion** and debate the ideas. What are the pros and cons? Start to think about solutions to the concerns.

Eliminate some ideas, shortlist others.

Feedback ideas and concerns

Step 3: Look for emerging proposals

Is there one idea, or a series of ideas, that brings together the best qualities of what has been discussed? Look for a solution that everyone might agree on and create a proposal.

Feedback ideas, concerns and proposals from other groups

Step 4: Discuss, clarify and amend proposal

Taking into account all the other groups' positions as well as those within your own group. Ensure that any remaining concerns are heard and that everyone has a chance to contribute.

Look for **amendments** that make the proposals even more acceptable to the whole group.

▼

Step 5: Test for agreement

Check for blocks, stand asides, reservations and active agreement.

Feedback position of each small group

No? **Check if decision has been reached**

Yes?

Step 6 Consensus! Implement the decision.

Decide who will do what, when it needs to be done by, and if necessary, how it should be done.

Example: a spokescouncil in detail

The following example outlines the consensus process for a spokescouncil. The groups in this example go through this process looking at one issue at a time, since this is the simplest way to do it. However, to speed things up, the groups could have decided to take several issues at once. Also, steps 1 and 2 can take place in advance within the individual small groups.

Question: *shall several groups join together in some kind of network or alliance?*

1. As a whole group: Introduce and clarify issue.

Facilitators explain consensus and spokescouncil process to the assembled small groups:

"We're going to be using consensus decision making between all the groups here today. Consensus is a way of making decisions together in a way that everyone is happy with the outcome: to reach a decision everyone has to give their consent for a proposal to be passed. We'll be using the following process to discuss items on the agenda. *[Describe process to be used, including ways of agreeing and disagreeing, and the roles of the facilitator(s)]*.

"We'll be communicating with each other using the spokescouncil system. At each stage of the discussion we'll nominate someone from the group to be a spoke for us, and someone to be our note-taker in the spokescouncil. Our spoke won't make decisions for us, just explain to the other spokes what we have agreed in this group. The note-taker will observe and take notes, so everyone will know what is being said in the spokescouncil, and this leaves our spoke free to concentrate on representing our views accurately.

"The spokescouncil will listen to all the views and decisions from the groups, and possibly make some proposals on how to move towards a common decision. When they've done this, our spoke and note-taker will come back to us and tell us where other groups are at, and about any suggestions or proposals from the spokescouncil. We'll think about this, come to some decisions or make some suggestions, and send our spoke and note-taker back to the spokescouncil again. This will go on until we all reach consensus."

A Consensus Handbook

The facilitators introduce the issue to be decided and give (or ask someone else to give) all the necessary information for making an informed decision. Make time for clarification.

Facilitators clearly define the question(s) for decision:

"So, we're deciding on whether all the groups here today are going to join together in some kind of alliance. Everyone here today is working on migrant support in our city, and so far, we've all agreed that by working together on publicity and fundraising we can have a bigger impact. So now the question is how we want to work with the other groups that are here today on these two areas: on publicity and funding?"

2. In small groups: Explore the issue and look for ideas.

Everyone voices their initial thoughts and reactions. What are the issues and concerns arising from the matter? You could use tools such as go-rounds or paired listening in the small groups to ensure everyone is heard:

"Let's do a go-round to hear everyone's initial views on this..."

If the issue raises strong emotions or impacts very strongly on the people involved, it is very helpful to take a break from the small group and use the spokescouncil for feeding back the concerns between the different groups, so that everyone can take other groups' views into account when discussing ideas:

"OK, so far we've heard some strong views on fundraising. We discussed these issues, and decided that our group would only be happy with a network wide funding bid if it complies with the ethical

standards of all the groups in the network. We should feed that into the spokescouncil meeting, so that everyone else can consider it."

Next, move on to coming up with ideas for possible solutions in your small groups. Use tools like go-rounds or ideastorms (see Chapter 6: Facilitation techniques and activities).

Then the small groups discuss the ideas they've come up with. What are the pros and cons? Some ideas get discarded at this stage, and new ideas may be formed:

"OK, so we've let everyone else know that there may be an issue around fundraising. While they're considering that let's have a think about how the network could do fundraising in a way that everyone can be happy with."

3. In the spokescouncil: Look for emerging proposals.

The facilitators call the spokes to the spokescouncil. Here, each spoke takes a turn to present the views of their group, covering the breadth of ideas and concerns as well as possible ways forward:

"We've heard from the various spokes about the variety of opinions on the fundraising issue. Some groups have quite strict ethical criteria on which grants and funds they want to apply for, and others are quite relaxed about it all. So far it doesn't seem that anyone is opposed to the idea of limiting our funding options – at least for grant applications made in the name of this network.

"Let's check back with our groups that this is the case: that everyone is actually happy to have some kind of commonly agreed restriction on funding applications. If that is the case then we can start working out our agreement on how to actually do it..."

"OK, we've all checked in with our groups, and everyone is happy

A Consensus Handbook

with the idea of making some kind of agreement on who we can apply to for funding, and what for. Does anyone have any ideas from their groups to share?"

The spokes then have a discussion to try and incorporate the various possible ideas into one synthesised proposal, or the facilitators might spot possible areas of agreement. During this process the spokes may call 'time out' to confer with their group for clarification or to see whether a modified proposal would be acceptable to them.

4. In small groups: Discuss, clarify and amend proposals.

The spokes report back to their groups on the discussion in the spokescouncil and present the concerns of the other groups plus possible proposals:

"So the suggestion from the spokescouncil is that we set up a subgroup to check in with each group in the network and come up with a proposed funding policy for us all to agree at the meeting next month. What do we think about that in our group?"

The groups discuss the proposal(s) and modify them if necessary:

"Right, so we're going to suggest a modification to the proposal. We think that the policy shouldn't be set in stone, but needs to develop as the network grows, to reflect any changes in the groups. So we suggest that a working group looks at the policy at least once a year, and brings any proposed changes to a full meeting for consideration by all the groups."

5. In small groups: Test for agreement.

Check for blocks, stand asides, reservations and active agreement. If there are major concerns about a proposal try to come up with ideas on how it could be resolved for your group. Work out the range of proposals that would be acceptable to your group:

"We're happy with the idea of the funding policy being reviewed regularly, but are worried that it'll always be the same people doing that, they may not be representative of all the groups in the network. So we'd be happy with anything between:

a) people on the funding policy are regularly chosen in some way, such as chosen at random, or agreed by everyone; or

b) every group is represented in some way on that working group."

6. In the spokescouncil: Check whether decision has been reached.

Spokes meet back at the spokescouncil and facilitators check whether groups agree. If not all groups agree, the discussion continues and new proposals are formulated using the information about what alternatives groups would be willing to agree to:

"Right, so no group has a problem with the funding policy group having a shifting membership, but some groups are worried that selecting people might take up a lot of time if it is done in a network-wide meeting. So the proposal to take back to our groups is that each group nominates one of their members to be in the policy group."

7. In small groups or the whole group: Implement decision.

If consensus has been reached, the decision is implemented by all. Remember to decide who will do what and to set deadlines.

Variations of a Spokescouncil

Fish bowl

To make the spokescouncil more accountable and reduce the need for repeating information, it can take place in the *fish bowl* format (see graphic), with the groups sitting in an outer circle around the spokes. Each group sits directly behind their spoke, which makes it easier for the spoke to quickly check back with their group. Just as in other forms of the spokescouncil, only the spokes should speak (apart from in small group discussion time).

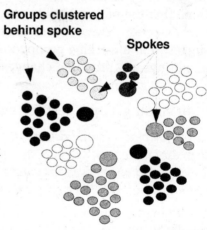

Groups clustered behind spoke

Spokes

Tiered spokescouncils

Even spokescouncil meetings are limited in size – when there are more than 20-40 spokes or small groups another tier might be needed.

In this case each spokescouncil sends a spoke to a second or even third level spokescouncil. With this number of people it becomes even more important to think carefully about which decisions actually need to be made by everyone and which can be left to individual groups. Each additional tier adds more time to the process. This can work for many thousands people, e.g. 9000 people involved in the blockade of a Castor nuclear waste transport in 1997. However, quite often the tiered spokescouncil is used as a channel for information and consultation rather than being used for actual decision-making.

Long-distance spokescouncils

Where there are groups of people in different locations they can use the spokescouncil model for long-distance decision-making. Rather than all members of all groups converging in one place to make a decision, groups can discuss the issue at home and then send a spoke to a meeting. The spokes comes back with a proposal that the groups either accept or amend. The problem here is that of time delay.

There are two ways around this – groups can be meeting in their home towns at the same time as all the spokes are meeting. The spokes ring or email any emerging proposals to the groups for discussion and feedback.

The second option is that spokes talk to each other on the phone or via internet chat and email. This needs good facilitation and the use of appropriate on-line tools, see: Chapter 4: *Facilitating consensus in virtual meetings.*

Chapter 4:
Facilitating consensus in virtual meetings

Meetings can be quite challenging – and if you're not all in the same place they can be harder still. If you can't see each other or the facilitator you'll be missing out on the non-verbal cues you'd normally be able to pick up through body language. This makes it harder to build trust and respect in the group. To make such meetings work everyone needs to work harder to express themselves clearly, and to understand each other.

Why have virtual meetings?

For most of us the easiest way to discuss and decide on an issue is when we're in the same place, and are all able to see and hear each other. But this isn't always possible: perhaps someone is working away from home but still wants to be involved, or your group might be made up of people from different countries. Perhaps you're sharing a project with another group that isn't based locally. If you still want everyone to be able to participate in your decision-making then you'll need to find a way to communicate with each other – we're calling this a **virtual meeting**.

In this chapter we'll be exploring some options for how to make decisions online and using the phone. We've included some pros and cons of the various options, and suggested a process for reaching consensus remotely.

The tools for the job

Before we talk about how to facilitate virtual meetings we'll take a short look at what communications media are available. Lots of the tools you can use to hold virtual meetings are based on the internet. We've tried to talk about these tools in a general way, because technology and software changes so quickly that what we write here will soon be out of date (but we've included some examples since most people know the name of the software they use, rather than the type of communication it is).

Chat: real-time text based messages over the internet, including IRC and Instant Messaging (IM). *MSN, IRC, AIM, Pidgin*

Collaborative real-time editors: software that allows more than one user to simultaneously edit a document. *Etherpad, Piratepad, Googledrive*

Email: sending digital messages to one or more recipients in non-real time.

Microblogging: a way to broadcast short messages to others. *Twitter, Identi.ca*

Post/Mail: sending old fashioned letters through the postal service.

Telephone: whether mobile or landline, also radio (CB, VHF etc.).

Voice Messages: leaving a message on something like an answerphone, or sending voice recordings via the internet or post.

VOIP: strictly speaking part of the telephone service, but here we use it to mean voice communications using computers rather than just telephones. *Skype, Mumble, google Talk*

Wiki: a website on which users can add, modify, or delete content using a web browser. *we.riseup.net*

Pros and cons of using these tools are discussed below.

Challenges of facilitating virtual meetings

Facilitation is about helping a group to have an efficient and inclusive meeting. Facilitating a virtual meeting is a bit more challenging than a meeting where everyone is physically present, but relevant tools and a bit of practice should make it easier.

Trust and understanding

When we phone, chat, email or collaborate on an online document it's very easy to lose sight of the fact that we're dealing with other humans. This is because we're missing out on most non-verbal communication: some researchers conclude that 70% of communication between humans is non-verbal (such as body language and tone of voice). Email doesn't allow us to express tones of voice or emotions, and telephones don't show us when people are frowning or smiling.

Virtual meetings are often easier when people have already met each other in real life – meeting up *helps* us get a picture of each other, *helping* us to trust, understand and respect each other better. Meeting up face to face at least occasionally can really help keep communications on a human level. You should also put some time aside to check on how everyone is feeling at the start of any meeting, so people have a chance to reconnect to each other.

Developing clear, shared aims in your group will help all participants to focus in meetings, as well as feel connected. Try to sort out common aims as soon as you can – this could be one thing you try to do as a group in one place, or failing that, use some of the collaborative software and internet sites to work together on them.

Preparation

As with any meeting, preparation really makes a difference. If people aren't meeting face to face it's probably even more important to think beforehand about what needs to be sorted out.

A Consensus Handbook

Whatever technology you're using for your meetings – whether it's the postal service or super complicated multi-media collaboration software – it pays to have clear systems for your facilitation and decision making.

As a facilitator, your first task will be to check the time scales for any decision making. If you're all going to be communicating in real time (such as on the phone) have you checked the times of the day that participants can or can't do – consider things like work, child-care, access to the internet and time zones.

If a meeting is to happen using non-real time communication (such as email) has a schedule been set for each stage of the discussion? Do people know when they should reply by?

Has everyone got access to the hardware (computers, cameras, microphones) and software (internet browser, apps or programmes)? Are all the different versions of software being used compatible?

At the same time as you're agreeing meeting times or time-scales, make sure that everyone has all the information they need to make the decision: are the agenda, minutes from previous meetings, information materials etc. available to everyone?

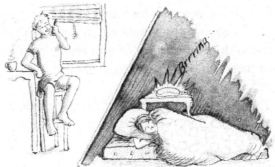

Real time or non-real time?

Real time communications happen when you and somebody else can immediately respond to what is being said, so the flow of conversation is faster.

But if you have to wait for a response, then this is called **non-real time**. Although it's generally not as convenient to communicate in non-real time, it can allow people more time to think, or for them to contribute at a more fitting time.

Facilitation styles

Facilitating virtual discussions in real time will often benefit from very clear facilitation – the kind that in a face-to-face meeting might feel over the top. Because we can't take visual cues from each other and the facilitator it's easy for people to talk over each other and go off on tangents. By explicitly explaining what they are doing, the facilitator can help the group to understand where the discussion is at and when they should speak or type.

Although in a 'normal' face-to-face meeting things like breaks, regular summaries and clarity about the process are important, when you can't see each other these things are perhaps even more important, but easier to forget about. So do:

★ plan in regular breaks – it can be more difficult to concentrate at a virtual meeting than at a real meeting. Split up the meeting into sections if necessary;

★ summarise lots – it's so easy to lose the thread of an email or chat based discussion (mix your media – if you are using VOIP, post summaries on a wiki: this reminds everyone where things are in the discussion);

★ keep an eye open for people who aren't contributing – it's very easy to overlook quiet participants when you can't see them;

★ only discuss one thing at a time – if you are using a wiki give each item its own page, on email each item should have its own (relevant and clear!) subject header;

★ If using real time tools, take names of the people who wish to speak before the next person starts their contribution.

Your group's structure

Before you set up elaborate systems for your virtual meetings think about how to minimise the amount of meeting time you'll need, for example it can be much harder to make decisions in virtual meetings with lots of people. If you can split up into working groups (e.g. publicity, venue organising, materials) then not everyone has to discuss everything. Instead only the few people in a particular working group will be meeting – helping to keep virtual meetings smaller and easier.

Pros and cons of different communications media

Real time spoken communication

VOIP, phone conferences – *everyone 'present' at the meeting.*

Pros and cons

✓ Possibly feels the most 'natural' of all the communication tools.

✗ Minutes need to be taken by a human.

✗ Phone and internet access can be expensive.

✗ Latency (time lag) and echoing can be off-putting.

Tips and troubleshooting

★ Before starting the meeting remind participants not to put the call on hold if their phone has hold music or beeps.

Real time written (typed) communication

Chat – *everyone 'present' at the meeting.*

Pros and cons

✓ Easy to use – quite a simple technology.

✗ People who can type faster tend to dominate the discussion

Collaborative editors (whether or not used in real time)

Everyone 'present' at the meeting or looking at the discussion when there's time.

Pros and cons

✓ Most collaborative software includes a chat client – useful for instant feedback and to discuss wording.

✓ Easy to save discussions, so no need to keep minutes.

✗ Hard to watch out for quiet participants.

Non-real time written communication

Email, email lists, forums, wiki, blogging, text/SMS, post – *no need for people to be 'present' at the meeting.*

Pros and cons

✓ Allows for a deeper debate since people have more time to think about their answers – there's more time to identify the best proposals and ideas.

✓ Leaves a record which is relatively easy to search through at a later stage.

✓ The actual time each person is involved in the discussion can be shorter than in a face to face or internet chat type meeting.

✓ Easy to exchange information (such as agendas and background info) and more complex thoughts.

✗ People who have more time and access to the internet may dominate the flow of the discussion.

✗ Decisions can take longer to reach because of high latency (delay between replies).

✗ Easy for important and relevant bits to get lost in a sea of words – although a facilitator can help with regular and clear summaries.

Tips and troubleshooting

★ Contributions can be sent to the facilitator who sends a digest on a regular basis. That way inboxes don't fill up so rapidly.

★ The facilitator can send out summary messages every so often, including summaries of the discussion and any proposals or decisions. This makes it easier for people to catch up if they've been away from the discussion or don't have much time.

★ The facilitator should set a deadline for replies, but first consider people's availability and access to the internet and ensure everyone will get a chance to participate in the discussion!

★ In order to keep things moving you may agree that if people don't respond to proposals by set deadlines then it will be assumed they are in agreement. For important decisions the facilitator should check in with everyone who hasn't explicitly responded to confirm agreement, stand asides or whether they just weren't able to get to a computer.

Example Chat Meeting

An illustration of how a virtual meeting might be facilitated:

Facilitator: OK, so let's start. Just to recap the 'handsignals' we're using: if you want to speak, put your hand up by typing H.

Facilitator: If you have a direct point, use HH for two hands.

Facilitator: I'll let you know when it's your turn to speak. Remember to type E for end when you've finished. So, let's start.

Facilitator: The first point on the agenda is agreeing on the location for the skillshare weekend. Does anyone know of a place we could use? e

Tom: h

Nancy: hh

Marianne: h

Facilitator: Nancy I see you have a direct response, then Tom and Marianne. e

Nancy: I've spoken to all the people who are planning to come. Can we ensure the place is accessible and child-friendly?

Facilitator: Nancy have you finished? Please remember to put an e when you have finished. e

Nancy: e

Tom: The place I know about is not accessible. e

Sara: h

Facilitator: Marianne then Sara. e

Case study: Virtual meetings in practice

The International Women's Peace Service (IWPS) is an organisation that is run by volunteers coming from all around the world. Meetings and decisions are made over the internet and the phone. In this way the internet and the phone becomes the 'office' where thinking, discussions and decisions are made and implemented.

Most decisions are made by email; a new email thread with the information is sent out when anything comes up, asking for people's thoughts and reactions. The person who sends out the email facilitates the discussion until a decision is made.

When strategic or urgent core issues come up then a meeting is held. Meetings are held on real time written collaborative tools because of their user-friendliness. Two people volunteer to facilitate and take minutes. Those who cannot attend the meeting email their views in advance to the rest of the group.

If the meeting takes too long, the issue is passed back to the relevant working group who continue discussing through email until a proposal is reached.

Since volunteers come from different continents, finding a time that works for everyone proves to be tricky. Using non-real time tools allows everyone the flexibility to take in information and respond to it in their own good time. In cases of emergency or people not having regular internet access the facilitator uses the phone to get feedback and passes that on to the rest of the group by email.

All decisions made are saved onto a wiki which serves as a filing system, including policies that were agreed upon and how-to documents that explain the decision process and facilitation, facilitation tools and communication tools used.

A consensus process for virtual meetings

Step 1: **Introduce issue** *(at least the day before, but more time is better)*. Share background info, policy, previous decisions etc. Work out what the questions are, e.g. on a wiki.

▼

Step 2: **Explore the issue and look for ideas.** *Use any media your group feels comfortable with for this step.*
1. Gather initial thoughts and reactions. What are the **issues** and people's **concerns**?
2. Collect **ideas** for solving the problem – write them down.
3. Have a **broad ranging discussion** and debate the ideas. What are the pros and cons?
Start thinking about solutions to people's concerns. Eliminate some ideas, shortlist others.

▼

Step 3: **Ideas: collect and summarise**
Publish the ideas, summarise and synthesise as necessary, e.g. *by email, on wiki*

▼

► *Step 4*: **Discuss pros and cons of the ideas**

▼

Step 5: **Facilitator summarises, asks for proposals (synthesises** and **combines proposals** as necessary).
Look for a proposal that weaves together the best elements of the ideas discussed. Look for solutions that address people's key concerns.

▼

Step 6: **Proposals published, amendments invited and discussed.**
Ensure that concerns are heard and everyone has a chance to contribute – seek feedback from all participants.
Look for amendments which make the proposal even more acceptable to the group.

▼

Step 7: **Test for agreement** – *if no agreement back to step 4*.
Do you have agreement? Check for the following:
Blocks: There is a fundamental problem with the core of the proposal that has not been resolved. We need to look for a new proposal.
Stand asides: I can't support this proposal because ... But I don't want to stop the group, so I'll let the decision happen without me.
Reservations: I have some reservations but am willing to let the proposal pass.
Agreement: I support the proposal and am willing to implement it.
Consensus: *No blocks, not too many stand asides or reservations? Active agreement?*
Then we have a decision!

▼

Step 8: **Implement the decision**
Who, when, how? Action point the tasks and set deadlines.

Chapter 5:
Quick consensus decision making

So what do we do when we need to make a decision – fast? In dynamic situations such as actions and protests people may only have (at most) a few minutes to decide what to do. There are shortcuts to reaching consensus quickly in such situations, but it takes preparation and practice to do well. Nevertheless quick consensus is worth trying out because it's a way of making the best decision you can in the short time you have. If done well, it ensures that everyone actively agrees to the decisions taken and bears equal responsibility for the consequences.

Preparing for quick consensus

Quick consensus works best in groups that know each other well, work together and are committed to using consensus. The key to quick consensus is to skip the discussion stage of your decision making process, moving straight from introducing the issue to checking agreement on a proposal. But since the discussion stage is the most important part of the decision making process it can only work if your group takes the time in advance to explore each others' needs and likely reactions in the situations you might meet. In effect, this is like having the discussion stage of the usual consensus process in advance. The better people in your group know each other, the more likely it is that you'll be able to anticipate what is likely to work for everyone in a given situation.

You can start by thinking up the likely scenarios, e.g. you might find yourselves needing to decide quickly whether to stay in a demo that is turning violent. Discuss these scenarios in depth with your group, then have a few practice quick consensus decisions. Give yourselves a time limit to come to a decision on relevant scenarios, e.g. "You're taking part in a march. The police have given you two minutes to get out of the road, or they'll arrest you all. What do you do?"

If the group is newly formed, or there's not much time before the situation in which you might need to use quick consensus then it's definitely worth prioritising getting to know each other and sharing information and feelings.

Preparation tips

It's pretty much essential for everyone in your group to share in advance how they feel about the different situations that may happen.

Think about how accurately you can you guess likely behaviour in various situations:

★ What might affect your behaviour?
★ What makes you stressed? Or chilled?
★ Is there anything people in the group should know about you? E.g. you're asthmatic and react badly to tear gas; you get aggressive easily if you see police mistreating someone or you get freaked out in chaotic situations.

If you think you may be in a situation where quick consensus may not work, for example you won't have any time at all to make a decision, or you haven't been able to do the right preparation then your group should think (in advance!) about other ways of making decisions, whether that's following a particular person's lead or a pre-arranged general plan.

Who's the facilitator?

Since efficiency is one of the keys to quick consensus, it's sensible to agree on a facilitator prior to going into any situation. There are lots of ways to choose your facilitator: they may be the person with the most relevant experience in that situation, or perhaps the person who is most alert on the day.

How it works

The following approach assumes you have only a minimal amount of time to make a decision. If you have a bit more time then you may wish to include some discussion, but the facilitator will have to decide at the time.

When you need to make a decision quickly, it is the role of the facilitator to summarise all that has happened and clarify the decision that needs to be made.

After the summary, move straight onto making just *one* proposal. If the group is considering more than one proposal then it'll take time to discuss which to use, or how to synthesise the various elements. By having just one proposal at a time you can keep the process simple and quick.

Once everyone has understood the current proposal, check first whether anyone is blocking it. If it is blocked, then move onto another proposal immediately, rather than spending time on discussing the block. On the other hand, if you hit upon a proposal that will work, then simply go with that.

If there is time, check for stand asides. If stand asides happen then you can ask for amendments to improve the proposal which might help everyone to feel comfortable with the proposal in its entirety. The facilitator's role is then to move the discussion on to implementing the decision.

Outline of quick consensus

1) Appoint a facilitator in advance.

2) The facilitator briefly states the situation to make sure everyone is clear: *"We've been given two minutes to move off the road or we'll all be arrested."*

3) The facilitator asks for proposals. In some cases there may be time for discussion, but in others there won't be. It's up to the facilitator to assess the time and act appropriately.

4) Someone makes a proposal: *"Yeah, I propose we link arms and sit down."* (In some cases you might have time to make amendments to the proposal.)

5) Facilitator restates the proposal, for clarity, and then tests for consensus:
"It's proposed that we sit in the road and link arms. Any Blocks?"
"No..."
"Any standasides?"
"Yeah, I'll lose my job – I want to leave."
"OK, anybody willing to go with Jo?"
"Yes, I will."
"OK, we're agreed!"

6) Make sure everyone knows who is doing what – and then get on and do it!

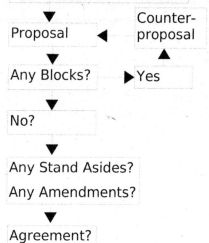

Facilitator summarises the situation and clarifies the decision that needs to be made.

Proposal ◀ Counter-proposal

Any Blocks? ▶ Yes

No?

Any Stand Asides?

Any Amendments?

Agreement?

Blocks and stand asides

As with the usual consensus processes, there is a difference between blocks and stand asides.

Blocks are more likely to happen in quick consensus because the group hasn't had time to explore where people are on the decision.

A **stand aside** means "I won't do this but I'm OK if the rest of the group does it". This allows the proposal to go ahead in the group's name, but those that choose to stand aside take no part in that action.

A block kills a proposal – it's a total veto.

Everyone has the right to block. It means: "I don't want the group to do this". In quick consensus people normally block for two reasons:

★ a proposal will split the group, often because some people have an ethical objection to it, or because it might endanger someone's safety; or
★ the group is failing to make a decision, and the discussion is taking time. The whole point of quick consensus is that it's quick, so you may find one participant blocking so that a new proposal can be considered: if a proposal is blocked, you need a new one!

Some groups insist that in quick consensus you must have a counter proposal before you can block.

Guidelines for quick decision making

Some tips to help make quick consensus work.

★ Active agreement – consciously participating in the decision, and showing agreement (e.g. by using hand signals) – if there isn't active agreement, you need to ask "Is there really any energy for this idea?"

★ One voice at a time – avoids discussion descending into chaos.

★ Handsignals: a number of hand gestures can speed up the process of decision making. For them to be effective, everyone in the group must know them, so agree them in advance! You want to minimise the number of handsignals you use and pare it down to essentials, e.g.:

☆ Raise a finger: "I'd like to speak."

☆ Hands waving with fingers upwards: "I support the idea currently being discussed", "I agree."

☆ Fist: "I block this proposal."

Chapter 6:
Facilitation techniques
and activities

This is a compilation of techniques and activities for facilitating consensus and participatory meetings. They are categorised according to when in the meeting you might want to use them – at the start, during the discussion, at the end, or in the middle to re-energise people. However, many of them can also be useful in other contexts.

Some general guidelines for using these tools:

★ **Every group is different**: some tools may not be appropriate in a specific group or situation. Don't force a tool on a group or an individual but let people decide for themselves to what extent they want to participate.

★ **Be flexible**: don't let your choice of tool dictate what happens, but fit and adapt the tools to the needs of the group. Be creative and invent your own tools.

★ **Use visual aids** such as flipcharts and whiteboards. Use them to write down instructions, questions and responses.

★ **Confidentiality**: be aware that people might not be happy to share everything that was said in a pair or a small group with all the people in the room.

★ **Explain the purpose of a tool** before asking the group to use it. That way people feel in control of what they are doing, allowing them to participate more fully.

Starting the meeting

Giving participants a chance at the start of a meeting to get to know each other, find out how everyone is feeling and set out the basics for how the meeting will run all help to build a rapport. This can really help ensure a positive flow and atmosphere in a meeting.

The following techniques can be used at the beginning of the meeting to create an open trusting atmosphere and for developing a respectful meeting culture.

Help people to get to know each other and build trust

Successful consensus decision-making is based on trust between people involved. Trust takes time to build and a big part of it is getting to know each other. This involves devoting some time to finding out what is going on in people's lives, talking about events that have shaped us, sharing how we are feeling and what's important to us.

There are lots of different ways of doing this and we mention just a few common techniques in this chapter – you can find lots more activities on the internet by searching for trust building exercises.

A simple and effective step is to ask people to introduce themselves at the beginning of each meeting. You could do this in the whole group by asking everyone to take turns to give their name, and some other information, for example: where they are from, what kind of food they like, why they are at the meeting or something good that happened in the last week etc. Alternatively you could ask people to pair up with someone they don't know, or know less well. One person interviews the other for three minutes, then roles are swapped. Questions can include the reasons why the person is there and what they are hoping to learn or achieve during the meeting. When the whole group re-forms the pairs introduce each other, giving as much detail as they can remember. The facilitator could also suggest specific themes to be included in the interview.

Getting present

Often people bring a lot of external stresses and emotions to meetings. It is very helpful to make time for people to arrive, to share how they are feeling in general and help them focus on the meeting. One way of doing this is to ask each person in turn to share concerns, distractions and events that are on their mind. Ask everyone else to give their full attention to the speaker. For example: "I'm giving a presentation this afternoon and I feel nervous." "My daughter had a baby last week. It's my first grandchild." As facilitator you can help people if they appear stuck by asking questions such as: "Is there any action you want to take?" "Is there anything else you want to say about that?"

A variation on this is to ask people to share something good or exciting that has happened to them recently or since the last meeting. Both techniques also help build trust and understanding by putting people more in touch with each other's lives.

Drawing up a group agreement

It can be very useful to start your meeting by negotiating a group agreement. The aim of a group agreement is to create a safe and respectful space in which people can work together productively. It sets the tone for how people will behave in the meeting. Making an agreement together as a group about how people should behave in the meeting is far more empowering than having a facilitator set out 'rules' for everyone to follow. People are much more likely to respect and implement such an agreement – and it will make the facilitator's job much easier. When problems arise facilitators can refer back to this agreement, e.g. "We all agreed at the beginning that it's best if only one person speaks at a time..."

How to create a group agreement

There are lots of ways to create group agreements. How much time you spend on it will depend on whether the group will be working together in the longer term, how controversial the topic of the meeting is, how much time you have and what level of trust the group have in the facilitator.

Start by asking everyone to think about: "What things would make this group/meeting work well for you?" or "What makes this a safe and respectful place for us to work in?"

People can respond by calling out points to be written up on flipchart paper or they could write comments on pieces of paper and group them together on the wall. Alternatively people could talk about the question in pairs or small groups and then feed this back to the whole group.

Once a list of suggested points has been compiled, the facilitator should, if necessary, ask for clarification on points and discuss how it can be turned into practical ways of working. E.g.:

★ "'It's OK to disagree' – how would this work practically? What about adding: '... by challenging what a person says, not attacking the person themselves.'"

★ "'Confidentiality' – what do people understand by that? What level of confidentiality do we expect from the group?"

Finally the facilitator needs to check for agreement on all the points from the whole group. It's good to make sure it's on display for all to see – written up on a whiteboard, flipchart paper or overhead projector.

If there's not enough time for this process, the facilitator could propose a group agreement, such as the one in the sidebar, then seek additions, amendments and then agreement.

Sample group agreement

1. Make sure everyone is able to contribute: more talkative people: show a little restraint; quieter people: your contributions are very welcome.

2. Only one person speaks at a time: put up your hand if you want to speak and wait for your turn.

3. Respect each others' opinions even and especially if you don't agree with them.

4. Participate!

5. Confidentiality – some things shouldn't be repeated outside of this meeting.

6. Be conscious of time – help stick to it, or negotiate for more.

7. Mobile phones off to minimise disruptions.

8. Regular breaks.

9. Active agreement – everyone to actively signal their opinion on any given issue.

Regulating the flow of the meeting

Using hand signals

Hand signals can make meetings run more smoothly and help the facilitator see emerging agreements.

Three simple signals should suffice:

Raise a hand when you wish to contribute to the discussion with a general point. Wait until it is your turn to speak.

Raise both hands if you want to add directly relevant factual information which people need to hear before other points. This allows you to jump to the head of the queue. Examples of appropriate use include providing a factual correction or answering a factual question. E.g.: "Shall we get the bus at 10 or 11 tomorrow?" A direct response would be: "The buses are on strike tomorrow," or possibly "The 11 o'clock bus arrives after the film starts," but not: "Personally, I'd prefer to get there a bit earlier, because..." In other words, the direct response doesn't give you the right to jump the queue to have your say on the discussion topic!

Silent applause when you hear an opinion that you agree with, wave a hand with your fingers pointing upwards. This saves a lot of time since it allows the facilitator to guage opinion, and people don't need to chip in to say "I'd just like to add that I agree with..."

Keeping a speakers' list

Used in conjunction with hand signals (see above), it simply involves asking people to raise a hand when they wish to speak, and noting them down in order. They are then invited to speak in that order. The group will soon become impatient with people that ignore this protocol and just barge in and interrupt.

Talking stick

People may speak only when they hold the talking stick (or any other agreed object). This allows the person holding the stick to consider and take their time in voicing their views. It also helps make people conscious of when they interrupt others.

Parking space

 When something comes up that's not relevant to the discussion at hand 'park' it in the parking space (a whiteboard or large sheet of paper on the wall) and deal with it at an appropriate time later. This allows you to stay focused but reassures participants they will be heard. Make sure that you allow time on the meeting agenda to deal with parked items so that they don't just get forgotten!

Encouraging involvement

Our life experiences, personalities and cultural expectations influence how we participate in meetings. Some people will be more confident and able to voice their opinions, ideas and needs than others, which can lead to an imbalance in meetings. There are many ways in which we can encourage quieter people to get involved in the discussion. Below are a few techniques that are often used in consensus based meetings and have proved themselves well as ways to increase participation.

Go-rounds

Go-rounds can be used in many situations: for an initial gathering of opinions and ideas, to find out people's feelings, to slow down the discussion and help improve listening.

In a go-round everyone takes a turn to speak without interruption or comment from other people. Make sure that everyone gets a chance to speak. Allowing people to 'pass' means that no-one feels put on the spot.

It helps to establish clearly what the purpose or question of the go-round is – it may help to write it on a large sheet of paper for everyone to see. If your aim is to give everyone an equal say you can set a time limit for each person. If your primary concern is to air the issue it may be better to let people speak for as long as they want.

Ideastorming

This is a useful technique for quickly gathering a large number of ideas. It encourages creativity and free thinking.

Start by stating the issue. Ask people to say whatever comes into their heads as fast as possible – without censoring or discussion. This helps people to be inspired by each other's ideas. Make sure there is no discussion or comment on others' ideas – be especially vigilant about put downs or other derogatory remarks: structured thinking and organising come afterwards. Appoint one or two note takers to write all the ideas down where everyone can see them.

Once you have your ideas then you can start looking through the results. You may need to prioritise from the many options generated by the ideastorm – see below for ways of doing this.

Ideastorm variation

A roving ideastorm is a useful variation that gets the group physically moving. It also allows you to think about several different, but related, issues at once. Small groups each start at a different 'station' (a tabletop or wall space with a sheet of flipchart paper on it) and have a short ideastorm on that station's topic. You call time and they then move round the other stations ideastorming as they go. A short, well enforced time limit will keep the small groups moving and make this a dynamic experience.

Ask people to express their points clearly and to write legibly. Finish either with a group discussion or by sending groups back around the stations so they can read what other groups have added to the lists.

Splitting into small groups or pairs

There are lots of reasons to split into a smaller group for a discussion or a task: it can sometimes become difficult to discuss emotionally charged issues in a large group, or a large group may become dominated by a few people or ideas, stifling creativity and contributions from others.

Apart from these examples, many topics can be discussed more effectively in a smaller task group, and need not involve everyone – for example the details of laying out of the newsletter or organising the benefit gig. Smaller groups allow time for everyone to speak and to feel involved. They are a lot less intimidating and can provide a much more supportive atmosphere in which less assertive people feel more confident in expressing themselves. Think about the sort of group you need – a random split (e.g. numbering off) or specific interest groups? Explain clearly what you want groups to do. Write up the task where people can see it. If you want feedback at the end, ensure each group appoints a notetaker to report back and state what they need to feed back. You could also ask people to split into pairs.

Listening in pairs

This technique creates a space where people can explore and formulate their own thoughts and feelings on an issue without interruption. It helps people to gather and consolidate their thoughts both at the beginning of and during the consensus process. It can also help to uncover and resolve conflict.

In pairs, one person is the listener, the other speaks about their own thoughts and feelings on the issue. The listener gives full attention to their partner without interrupting. The listener can provide a supportive atmosphere through eye contact and body language and, if the speaker gets stuck, may ask neutral questions such as "How do you feel about that?" "Why do you think that?"

After a set time swap roles within the pairs. This exercise can be followed by a go-round in the full group, with every person summarising the thoughts of their partner.

Throwing questions back to the group

There's no need for facilitators to feel they have to deal with every problem that comes up in a meeting. Where possible, let the group do the work. If someone asks a question, the facilitator doesn't have to answer it, but can 'throw it back' to the group: "So we've had a suggestion that we break at around 3 o'clock – what do people think about that?"

A Consensus Handbook

Techniques for problem solving and tackling difficult issues

Below are some useful techniques for solving problems and tackling difficult issues. These generally benefit from strong facilitation, so do lay down clear rules and don't let discussions get out of hand. Don't be afraid to stop the process if necessary. If things get heavy then bear in mind that conflict resolution requires both skill and experience, and shouldn't be done unprepared. It's much better to stop the meeting and seek help from experienced facilitators.

Mapping

Use large writing on flipchart paper where everyone can see it and arrange key words in groups or out on their own. Connecting arrows, colours, pictures make this a lot more organic and fun than a simple list and it can allow people to make new connections. The writing could be done by one person or everyone in the group.

Using questions

Questioning involves asking the individual or group a question, or series of questions, to enable them to find their own solutions to the challenges they face. It can be used as an alternative to presenting information and answers as well as helping a group work their way through a problem and increasing the quality of a discussion. The increased interaction has the added benefit of keeping more people more deeply engaged in the meeting.

For example, the meeting that you're facilitating has just come up with lots of ideas for a community festival. Asking the group a series of questions will help them to narrow down these ideas to a few options to investigate further. Questions could include: "Which of these options fit with our objectives? How much time and energy are these going to need? What do we have most enthusiasm and energy for?"

Tips for successfully using questions:

✓ Have a clear aim. What are you trying to achieve? Ask questions that reflects this.

✓ Use open questions when you want to open up and explore issues. Use them to draw people out and to let them direct what is to be discussed. Open questions are questions that cannot be answered by a simple *yes* or *no* answer. They start with words such as "Who...?", "Why...?" or "What happened?", for example: "Who's going to take the minutes?", "When would you like to end the meeting?"

✓ Closed questions generally invite a *yes, no* or *don't know* answer. There is a place for closed questions when you want to clarify points, get information quickly or when you want to deliberately restrict options, for example "Would you like to stop for a break now?" rather than "How much longer do you need?"

✓ If you don't get a response to a broad question, break it down and ask a series of specific questions.

Sharing how people are feeling

Often we focus on practicalities and don't give ourselves enough time to think about our emotions. This can lead to people feeling unhappy or dissatisfied with a decision afterwards. When deciding an emotive issue it can be useful to build in an explicit step to find out how people are feeling about the discussion, ideas and proposals.

The facilitator should ask people to consider how they are feeling. Then have a go-round with people describing in a couple of words or sentences how they feel, for example: positive, nervous, tired, excited, disappointed and why they are feeling like this.

A Consensus Handbook

It's also possible to ask people to share any thoughts or emotions they have so far kept to themselves. These are usually things that are hard to express, things that are about how people are feeling about others in the meeting, or deep underlying needs and emotions. It can be difficult to create a climate in which people feel safe to express these.

Set up a go-round asking people to make statements beginning with: "What this proposal brings up in me is...", "What upsets me about this discussion is ...", "If I could change one thing in the group it would be...". Do not allow anyone to respond to people's statements or start a discussion. Make sure that everyone has a say – it is highly unlikely that everyone is completely happy with a group, discussion or meeting. At the end of the round, see if any themes have emerged and if anyone wants their issue discussed.

Spectrum lines

These help to explore the different views on an issue within the group. They are a dynamic way of discussing philosophical rather than practical topics in large groups. Make an imaginary or real line through the room. One end stands for "I agree completely", the other end for "I disagree completely". Outline the issue under debate and formulate it into a statement to agree or disagree with.

People should position themselves along the line according to their views, and be asked to have a short conversation with the person next to them, explaining why they are where they are. The next stage is usually to invite people to share their viewpoints and feelings with the group. Encourage people to shift their position along the line if they are influenced by what other people are saying.

If well facilitated, spectrum lines can inspire thought, listening and debate (both verbal and non-verbal). To achieve this it's important to think carefully about how to formulate the questions so that they're neither too shallow, nor too complex. Often the debate during a spectrum line needs strong facilitation so that people don't talk over each other.

Prioritisation techniques

These techniques are useful when you have several options and need to choose between them. *Show of hands* and *temperature check* are quick and easy methods to gauge group opinion so that you can rapidly drop unpopular ideas. The other methods allow you to investigate ideas in more detail.

Show of hands

Obvious, but effective. Run through your list or agenda and get a preliminary show of hands on how important each item is to the group. Those options that have less support are good candidates for being quickly scrapped. Remember to check with the people that made a suggestion before scrapping it – they might still want it to be discussed. It's also possible that an idea that's not popular at first glance can become the favourite after closer examination.

Temperature check

Another simple visual tool: ask everyone to stand and imagine a vertical axis with support for an idea at the top and no support at the bottom. Get them to stick out their hand and raise it along the imaginary axis for support (the higher the hand the more support) or lower it for opposition (the lower the hand the more opposition). If all the hands show a high temperature, you know the group the group likes the idea. If all of them are low down, you know people are feeling cool about it.

Stickers and dots

You can achieve a similar effect to the temperature check by giving everyone a number of stickers or dots (1–6 usually works). Write up a list of the ideas. Ask people to stick their stickers or make their dots by the item(s) that they consider to be most important for the group to deal with. If you give multiple dots or stickers, people have the choice of 'spending' them all on one item that they feel is really important or urgent, or spreading them across a number of options.

Pros and cons

Got several ideas and need to decide which one to go for? List the benefits and drawbacks of each idea in a table or map and compare the results. This can be done as a full group, or by asking pairs, or small groups to work on the pros and cons of one option and report back to the group. Be aware that what is a *pro* for one person might be a *con* for another – in this case you could write it down in both columns.

Facilitating prioritisation tools – a word of warning

It's easy to deviate from your process and get bogged down in endless discussion. What starts as an attempt to briefly list the pros and cons of each option can easily be diverted into a full scale hour long discussion on just the first option. Be wary of this, and stick to your chosen process. Only if the process itself is clearly not working should you abandon it and go for another!

Prioritisation, by definition, involves choosing some ideas over others. This means that throughout your prioritisation exercise you'll be discarding ideas. There are two possible pitfalls that you can easily avoid:

✗ The first is throwing away an idea too early, deciding later that you were too hasty, but not having written it down anywhere. So always note down ideas and keep hold of the notes until the decision is finally made. If new ideas arise, put them in the parking space.

✗ Secondly, people are usually more at-tached to the ideas that they thought of, so if you're facilitating, be wary of throwing ideas away too lightly and offending people. It can help to remind the group regularly that you're looking for ideas that are best for the group as a whole. You can also ask permission to discard ideas, and thank people for being willing to put aside their personal preferences.

You can also add another column called 'implications / interesting' where you can write down any implications, whether good or bad, or any interesting point.

You can extend the process by putting a score next to each plus – minus – interesting point. Then add up the columns – if the plus column scores highest the option is good. If the minus column scores highly look for a different option.

Urgent/important grid

A classic time-management tool that can be applied to group prioritisation! You can use this tool on paper, or as a spectrum line. The group ranks ideas according to their urgency and importance:

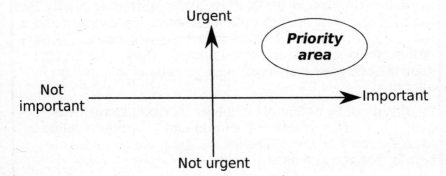

Ranking

This technique works well in combination with splitting into small groups. Write each option on a card or post-it note and give each group a full set of cards or post-its. Set a time limit and ask the groups to rank the options. It helps to set out clear criteria: "You've got 15 minutes. We are looking for options that need to be done most urgently, are most important yet realistic with our budget. And we've only got a week to make it happen."

Diamond ranking

This is a variation of the general card sorting tool. The group takes its 9 top ideas and sorts them into a diamond shape (see below).

Most support		1		
Next best ideas	2		3	
Other possibilities	4	5	6	
Little support	7		8	
Weakest idea		9		

Activities for re-energising

When people stop concentrating or become irritable in a meeting it sometimes just means they have been sitting and listening for too long. Simple things like a stretch, a game, or two minutes chatting to the next person can re-energise people. Games can also change the atmosphere in other ways – from lifting the spirits in the group to creating a quieter, more contemplative mood.

Be sensitive to the group and individual members – the idea is to help people feel better rather than embarrassed or isolated. Don't coerce people into playing games but respect their limits and boundaries. If people don't feel like playing, they could get themselves a cup of tea or go to the toilet. Also remember mobility issues. Sometimes a simple break or a stretch works just as well.

We've included a couple of games so you can see the kind of energisers that are commonly used. For more ideas for games and energisers have a look at our briefing *Facilitation Tools for Meetings and Workshops*, available from our website.

Knot game

Takes about 10 minutes; good for 10 – 20 people. Stand in a circle, close your eyes. Walk towards the centre of the circle with outstretched hands. Find another hand for each of yours. Then open your eyes. Unravel the knot without opening hands.

Involves getting physically close to others, stretching, laughing and problem solving. Make two simultaneous groups if there is a large number of people.

Who am I?

Takes min. 15 minutes; good for 5 – 10 people. Ask everyone to think of someone they admire who they could answer questions about, they should be known to most of the group. Keep it a secret. The group asks one person at a time questions about the person they admire until they guess it. The group gets three goes to guess the identity, if they don't get it in three attempts that person wins.

A Consensus Handbook

Evaluating meetings

Evaluation allows us to learn from our experiences. It should be a regular part of our meetings and decision-making processes as it gives us the chance for honest feedback on the process and each other's behaviour, allowing us to improve in the future.

Everyone who participated in a meeting should be encouraged to take part in its evaluation. Bear in mind that there will be differences of opinion and that it is not necessary for the group to come to agreement on the matter. It is important to point out what was successful as well as what could have gone better. Begin with positive evaluations wherever possible. The structure of the evaluation should be planned carefully – how will you draw out what type of information? Keep evaluations of the process and of the content of the meeting separate. Below are some possibilities:

★ Have a round where everyone sums up their feelings or ask everyone to write down comments on a large piece of paper.

★ Ask everyone to call out two or three high and low points of the meeting.

★ Draw up an evaluation questionnaire and distribute it amongst the participants for filling in.

★ Ask "What are you taking away from this meeting?" This rapid review can help people notice what they have achieved.

★ At the beginning, ask people to write their hopes and fears for the meeting on post-it notes and stick them on the wall. At the end ask them to take down any hopes that have been fulfilled and fears that have been dealt with or proved unfounded.

★ List the expectations that were gathered at the beginning of the meeting. To what extent were they satisfied or changed as the event progressed? Do the same with goals.

★ Use a graph on a large piece of paper representing the entire meeting. Each participant, using a different coloured pen, crayon or chalk, draws a line from one end to the other, drawing it above or below a central line depending on how much they enjoyed or gained from the session.

Chapter 7: Troubleshooting in your meetings

Like any method of decision-making, consensus isn't always easy to get right. **However, most of the sticking points stem from lack of experience, or because the conditions for consensus aren't being met** rather than there being a problem with consensus itself. It takes time to unlearn the patterns of behaviour we have been brought up to accept as the norm. Some of these problems, like unaddressed conflict or unhealthy power dynamics, may need long term action to sort out. Chapter 8: *Bridging the gap* provides some pointers on how to do this.

However, there are also things you can do in meetings, as a facilitator or a participant, which can make it easier to deal with issues that arise. For example, imagine that a small number of people do all the talking in your meeting. If you want to change this situation, you can start with looking at how power and

Facilitating problems

Step 1: actively listen for the underlying issue behind the problem.

Step 2: choose an appropriate facilitation technique to deal with the underlying issue.

Step 3: the underlying issue is dealt with and the problem is solved.

A Consensus Handbook

responsibilities are shared out in the group as a whole. But if you notice this happening in a particular meeting you will probably want to have some tactics up your sleeve to help others contribute in the short term as well. This chapter helps you pick the right tactics to deal with issues as they arise.

Even if you are just looking for a short term solution in a meeting, it is important to get to the bottom of the underlying issues. Probably the most important thing to do as a group is to take the time to reflect on how your consensus process is going, give each other feedback and constantly look for ways to improve. Develop your ability to spot problems and possible reasons behind them. Use your observations as a guide to find ways to deal with them. There are a handful of really common problems, but there are many possible issues underlying them. The approach you take will need to depend on the cause of the problem. Don't just ask "What's happening?" also ask "Why is it happening?" The more trust and understanding there is in a group the easier it will become to overcome such problems. Facilitation can help by supplying the tools to avoid problems in the first place and to deal with them creatively if they do occur.

Below we've compiled ideas for dealing with the most common issues that crop up in consensus based meetings.

Our meetings take a long time how can we speed things up?

Reaching good consensus decisions can take longer than voting, especially when a group is new to it. It can take time to look at and think about ideas until all objections are resolved – some decisions might take more than one meeting to decide. However, the advantage of consensus is that decisions are usually of a higher standard, and are more likely to stand the test of time. Bad decisions may not take as long to make in the first place, but they often need revisiting, or never get implemented. Decisions that don't have the full support of the group can cause resentment to bubble up in later meetings, leading to conflict which takes time to resolve. Consensus does get quicker with practise, particularly in a long-term group.

Saving time in consensus:

★ Make sure in advance that you have all the information you need at the meeting. Ideally, everyone should get up to speed before the meeting. If vital details are missing, work out what you need to find out, and when by, then move on.

★ Not every decision needs to involve the whole group. Delegate the nitty-gritty business to working groups (e.g. publicity or fundraising).

★ Split the meeting into parallel working groups to deal with several issues at once. Each working group could come back with various proposals for the whole group to decide on.

★ After a complex discussion get a small group, or even a pair, to go away and synthesise everyone's ideas into a few possible solutions to be discussed later by the whole group.

★ Good facilitation – keep the group focussed on the issue at hand. Stop people from going off on tangents.

★ Keep accurate minutes to avoid having to revisit decisions.

Time pressure

Feeling under pressure to find a solution to an problem leads to stress and a desire to 'just get on with it'. Be aware of the danger of reaching a consensus of the obsessed – when meetings run on for a long time, because a decision 'must be made today'; many people will tire, leave to go to bed or deal with childcare, and only those left at the end with the most stamina or strongest feelings will be involved in the final decision.

Be realistic about your meeting agendas. Try to make sure enough time is allowed in the agenda to tackle issues adequately. This might

A Consensus Handbook

mean delaying less urgent decisions, or allowing less important decisions less time. Check when the issue needs to be decided by – perhaps there's time for the meeting to be extended or continued another time? Could you find a temporary solution to be revisited when there is more time? Does the whole group have to be involved, or could a small group go away to discuss (and resolve) the issue, leaving everyone else to get on with the rest of the agenda?

Emergencies: there are ways of making consensus decisions in a very short time, but they take skill and practise and rely on the group having already spent time getting to know each other's views and needs (see Chapter 5: *Quick consensus decision making*). In an emergency you are aiming to make the best decision in the time you've got. In some cases appointing a temporary leader may be an expedient course of action. Obviously, you can appoint your leader and guidelines for their decisions in advance by consensus.

Our meetings lack focus

Sometimes meetings lack focus – several issues are being discussed at once and people keep going off on tangents. This can be very frustrating when you need to get some work done and make decisions. To avoid this draw up an agenda that outlines what will be discussed in what order and then stick to it. Appoint a facilitator to help the group to stay on topic and stop people from going off on tangents. If new issues come up in a discussion, acknowledge that they need discussing too, but separately. Make a note of them and schedule a time to discuss them.

Our group is large and we don't enjoy meetings

For groups of more than 15-20 people it is advisable to split into sub-groups for meaningful discussion. You can find more detail in Chapter 3: *Facilitating consensus in large groups*.

We're stuck and can't reach a decision

Do the conditions for consensus exist in your group?

★ Do you need to spend more time on developing **shared goals**? If you haven't agreed what the aims of the group are then spend some time doing that. If you can't agree on these, then maybe you need to consider splitting into different groups, or concentrating your work on any areas you do agree on.

★ Does everyone **understand how consensus works?** If not go through and explain both the process and the principles behind consensus decision making. Again, if some people aren't really committed to consensus, it might be better to make decisions in another way, or to split into two groups.

★ Do you have good **facilitation**? For tips on facilitation check Chapter 2: *Facilitating consensus*.

★ Is everyone able to be **open** about what they want, and what they actually need? If not, work out ways to build trust in your group to allow people to express themselves honestly.

★ Are people really **actively participating** in the process? Are they listening to each other? Is everyone trying to understand each other's standpoint, and work out how to accommodate each other's needs?

★ Are you spending enough **time** on your decision making? Bad decisions can often be made very quickly, but good decisions usually require listening and consideration – which can take time.

Chapter 8: *Bridging the gap* has more ideas on what to do in situations where the conditions for consensus aren't being met.

Can you actually make a good decision?

★ Do you have all the information you need to make a decision? If not, how can you get it?

★ Is the group unable to reach a decision because it has no good choices? Are you forced to choose between being shot and hung? In which case what options do you have for creating a situation where you can make real choices?

See Chapter 8: *Bridging the gap*, page 165 for more on how to deal with external pressures that make good decision making difficult.

Have you had an open, honest discussion about where people are coming from?

Sometimes the group has not gone deep enough in their discussion. People may be holding back from being completely open about their concerns and motives, or they might find it difficult to express them. Alternatively, it may be that someone hasn't been listened to carefully enough, and people are assuming they've understood when they haven't. Another common barrier to open, honest communication is difficult relationships between individuals that may make it harder for them to trust each other and open up, and to hear each other when they do.

Encourage everyone to explain their viewpoints in more depth. Listen carefully for agreements and concerns. What's at the root of people's worries? Which are the issues that are vital to address and which ones are side issues? Which areas does everyone agree on? Test for agreement periodically as this helps to clarify disagreements. Identify the common ground you think you can see and check if others see it too. It can help to state what you think the agreement is in the negative: "Is there anyone who does not agree that...?"

See Chapter 8: *Bridging the gap* for more on encouraging open, honest communication in situations where power dynamics or conflict pose issues. Also look at Chapter 1: *Making decisions by consensus*, page 31 for tips on active listening.

Has the discussion become polarised?

Groups can often be paralysed by individuals or factions holding strong conflicting positions. This can get to the stage where it looks like an either/or choice, with each option leaving one person or faction unhappy. This happens particularly easily if not enough thought and care has been put into the early stages of the discussion. For example if you introduce the issue as "Shall we cancel the event?" the only available options are *yes* and *no* and people are likely to come to loggerheads between them. You have a much better chance of finding a solution that works for everyone if you start by saying something like: "I'm concerned we're not well enough prepared for the event, what shall we do?", and take time to think up various options before you start to work out what your preferences are.

If the problems emerge later on, remind yourselves that consensus is about co-operating to find solutions and not competing. It's also essential to remember that holding onto our personal agendas and opinions is often an obstacle to this co-operation happening. So honest self-reflection is often needed. If the language of a discussion starts taking on tones of 'either/or', then take a break and look for other options. Can the ideas work together in any way? Are we falling out over small details and forgetting that we have a lot in common? There are rarely just two options, so be creative and think of new ways forward. You could ask everyone to argue convincingly the point of view they like the least. This might help people to understand the other side and make it easier to resolve conflict.

A Consensus Handbook

Do you really need to agree on this now or can you choose one of the options below?

★ Break down the decision into smaller areas. Are there any points on which you agree and can move forward? Can the other areas be resolved later?

★ Put the decision on ice: come back to it in an hour, a day or a week. Quite often when people have had a chance to cool off and think it through, things can look quite different. At other times people might just be too tired to see a way forward, in which case a break, an energising activity or even a cup of tea might help. If the decision is postponed it can sometimes be a good idea to facilitate conflicting parties in the meantime, to check for common ground and clarify wants and needs.

★ Imagine what will happen in six months, a year, five year's time if you don't agree. How important does the decision feel now? You might find that by putting it into context finding agreement becomes less (or more) important and people might be willing to shift their positions.

★ Agree an alternative process for taking a decision that all parties can sign up to. This could be allowing the person, or people, most affected to make the decision; putting all the possibilities into a hat and pulling one out; or simply tossing a coin. Some groups have majority voting as a backup, often requiring an overwhelming vote such as 80% or 90% to make a decision valid. Be careful not to turn to this at the first sign of trouble – it's a definite last resort in a consensus group.

Do you need an outside facilitator to help you through your sticky patch?

Sometimes it can help to bring in outside help. This needs to be done when there's still enough good feeling left for people to co-operate with the process and be willing to accept a different facilitator. Quite often an outside facilitator or mediator will be seen as neutral, which can help things along.

Is it time to split the group?

If the the group is continually divided over the same issues between the same people, it's probably a good time to think about the reasons for the disagreement. Should you really be acting together as one group? Do all members of the group share the same goals, and is everyone committed to reaching consensus? You might need to spend some time exploring these issues. Depending on the answers a group may ask members to leave, or may decide to split into two groups. Although this might be painful, it can be better for everyone in the long run. Ideally you'll carry on supporting each other and working together on shared projects.

Too many ideas?

Sometimes an issue brings up a large number of ideas. Groups naturally tend towards discussing them all at once which can be very confusing. Using facilitation techniques and activities, like listing pros and cons for each idea really helps keep discussion focused and give each idea a fair hearing. Look at Chapter 6: *Facilitation techniques and activities* and pick a process that gives space to hear each idea in turn and that allows it to be treated on its merits. Which parts of it work, which don't work so well for the group? Can you pick elements from different ideas to create one combined 'super-proposal'? Are there any ideas that can be filtered out – for example, ideas that go against the aims of the group? Can some of the proposals be delegated to working groups or sub groups for decision-making?

A Consensus Handbook

'Steamroller' proposals

Sometimes people already have firm ideas or proposals that they bring to the meeting. This could be from a working group (such as funding or publicity) or a local group in a network or an individual who has already spent some time thinking about the issue. Bringing proposals to a meeting can be helpful in speeding up the discussions. However there is a danger that the proposal will be pushed through without adequate discussion or modification. Also, people at the meeting often react negatively to a proposal because they have not had time to consider the matter for themselves and feel 'steamrollered', even if that was not the intention of the proposer.

To avoid these problems it's important to remind everyone that consensus is based on taking everyone's point of view into account, exploring different options and combining the best elements into a proposal. People bringing ideas to the meeting need to be willing to let the group modify and adjust them, maybe even beyond recognition.

Here are two ideas for dealing with pre-existing proposals:

Option 1. After explaining the issue to be discussed collect the existing ideas and put them to one side. Together explore the issue, gather concerns and look for any other new ideas. Add new ideas to your list. Have a broad ranging discussion about all ideas – the pre-existing ones and those that have come out of the meeting. Synthesise a proposal for consensus out of these.

Option 2. After explaining the issue to be discussed, outline the existing proposal. Together explore the issue itself and the pros and cons of the proposal. Make a list of people's concerns and other ideas. Modify the proposal to address these until everyone is happy with it. (This only really works if there is just one existing proposal. If there are two or more, using this process would set up an either/or dynamic that might make it really hard to reach agreement).

How can we deal with disruptive behaviour?

Do your meetings suffer from disruptive behaviour such as chatting, people arriving late and leaving early, incessant joking, and going off on tangents? Is there an issue with attention-seeking behaviour that regularly throws your meetings off track? This could be a sign that people's needs in the meeting are not being fulfilled.

All of us have some basic things we need in order to work in a group. We need to feel that we are being treated fairly. We need our expertise and experience to be valued and our ideas and opinions to be heard. We need to feel part of the group and we need to feel like we're getting something useful done. When these needs aren't fulfilled people can easily feel alienated from the meeting. This often expresses itself in disruptive behaviour. For example, they feel they had no say in the choice of agenda, and consequently can't see the relevance of what is being discussed. Or maybe they feel that the meeting is a waste of time because their opinion won't be considered when it comes to making the final decision.

Of course, disruptive behaviour can sometimes be the result of needs that are beyond our control, due perhaps to wider personal or societal issues. In this case, members of the group may do what they can to offer each other support over the longer term. In the the short term, the best option may be to use facilitation tools which keep the meeting on track and limit the impacts of attention-seeking behaviour (see below).

Alternatively the meeting might simply have gone on for too long, and people are tired and hungry and just need a break. It's also worth checking in with individuals as people's ability to sit still and focus varies. What feels OK to you might have gone on way to long for other people. Build in 15 minute breaks every 90 minutes or so and provide food and hot drinks for people to recharge.

Our group is dominated by a few individuals

A common form of disruptive behaviour in groups is when a handful of strong personalities do most of the group's talking and organising. Dominating behaviour can be very destructive for a group – it needs to be addressed if we are to achieve real consensus in meetings. Chapter 8: *Bridging the gap* has more on addressing power dynamics.

Dominant behaviour can be discouraged, and other people's participation can be increased with the use of a few simple facilitation techniques:

★ Reaffirm the group's commitment to openness and consensus at the start of meetings.

★ Gently remind dominant people that others also have valued opinions, and that meeting time is limited "Thanks for that contribution. It would be really nice to hear from anyone that's not yet had the chance to speak...." or, "Thanks, Tom, but do you mind if we let someone else speak now? Time's short and you've already spoken a few times..."

★ Use hand signals so that you can see who wants to speak, and prioritise those who haven't contributed so often.

★ Set up a group agreement that includes agreements not to interrupt, and to allow everyone a chance to speak.

★ Information is power. Share information at the beginning of the meeting through presentations and question and answer sessions. This means everyone is up to speed before the discussion starts.

★ Use go-rounds, small groups and paired listening to allow everyone to have a chance to speak.

★ Invite in a experienced facilitator, who will help highlight and deal with unhealthy group dynamics.

What to do when someone blocks

Why do blocks occur?

In an ideal consensus process a block wouldn't occur since any major concerns about a proposal would have been noticed and dealt with before moving on to the decision stage. The fact that someone feels the need to block a proposal means that something has gone wrong earlier in the process. But since this will sometimes happen, the option to block needs to be available. See Chapter 1: *Making decisions by consensus*, page 28, for more on the choices different groups make about what situations a block may be acceptable in.

Fundamentally, blocks occur when the conditions for consensus aren't being met. The kind of things that commonly go wrong, and end up with a block are:

★ The proposal goes against the agreed aims and principles of the group.

★ The proposal impacts in a profoundly negative way on an individual's fundamental needs.

★ An individual hasn't been able to express their concerns in a way that the group can understand, or maybe not at all.

★ Going ahead with the proposal would lead to severe consequences for individual members or the group, e.g. members leaving the group, either immediately or in the longer run; or serious legal or financial consequences.

★ The group is not ready to make a decision – more in-depth discussion is needed to address everyone's concerns and to involve everyone in the decision-making. There are many reasons for this, including: members of the group may be absent; not everyone had a chance to feed in their views; the proposal is being rushed through; people need time to think about it; vital information is missing.

What to do in case of block

Once someone has blocked, it is important for the whole group to understand the reasons behind it. Find out whether an amendment to the original problem might be satisfactory to everyone, otherwise go back to discussing other potential solutions to the issue.

It is also worth checking whether the block is actually a stand aside, as sometimes people don't understand the difference – but remember to be careful to avoid putting pressure on the person blocking when checking this. At the 'testing for consensus' stage of the meeting it can help to include a clear explanation of how your group uses the block (and other ways of disagreeing) and what it means: explaining this first avoids misunderstandings and the person who disagrees is less likely to take it personally than they would if their block was challenged.

Problems with blocks

There are three main issues connected to blocks, which we deal with below.

People are afraid to block

Making use of the block can be hard, especially for people who don't feel confident in their group. It can involve standing up to perceived or actual group pressure and impatience. Many people are tempted to keep quiet and important discussions are sometimes avoided.

Create an atmosphere in your meetings where people will feel able to block if necessary. This places particular responsibility on the facilitator in the decision stage to check what levels of agreement exist and to help people feel comfortable to speak up.

Misuse of the block

Because blocks are such powerful tools it's important to be aware of how they can be misused. Some of the common misuses are:

★ conscious or subconscious use of the block to maintain or gain power or attention;

★ different cultural and political backgrounds leading to

misunderstanding of the concept of the block;

★ the person blocking doesn't understand, or is not committed to, consensus. For example blocking when the proposal is still being discussed – i.e. not at the decision stage yet. This could either be because someone doesn't understand the process or because they have already made up their mind and are not prepared to listen and understand other people's positions and to modify their own.

If you feel a block is being misused:

★ Explain the consensus process and how the block works in your group. Do this at the beginning of meetings, and possibly again if a block occurs. This is especially useful when there are people new to the group or the group is very large.

★ Discuss the difference between a block and a stand aside. It may become clear that an objection is a stand aside rather than block. Be careful that the person blocking doesn't feel under pressure to stand aside.

★ If someone regularly blocks it may indicate that the group isn't meeting their needs – perhaps they don't feel listened to in discussions? Try to uncover such hidden dynamics and deal with them.

★ If someone finds themselves continually at odds with the rest of the group it may be time to consider whether this is the right group for that person. Does the person agree with everyone else about the aims and principles of the group? Would it be better for the person to leave?

People refuse to accept the validity of a block.

In some cases the rest of the group may be unwilling to respect a block. This is a difficult situation. A group should respect a block, unless it stems from a fundamental disagreement with the aims of the group, goes against what you have decided collectively about acceptable use of the block or is driven by abuse of power. It can be hard to work out if this is the case: it's hard to judge for someone else whether they really need something, or if they just want it, for example. Or one person might think that something goes against the core aims of the group, but others might not see it as so clear cut.

A Consensus Handbook

Some people argue that you should only be allowed to block a proposal if it is against the well-being of the group, however many groups feel it is valid to block for personal reasons. They argue that we need to respect each other even if we disagree profoundly – we can't just draw an arbitrary line to stop respecting people when it's about their personal view rather than the group's interest. For these groups commitment to consensus means carrying on looking for solutions for everyone, even when it becomes difficult.

If a group goes against a block this can completely undermine the member's commitment to the group and is against the principles of consensus. The fact that someone feels the need to block suggests that their concerns have not been taken into account. If that block is then not accepted by the group, this might be an even more serious sign that they are not being respected. This means that the conditions for consensus are not being met, and this needs to be addressed.

In the short term there are a few things you can do if a block is not being accepted:

★ In most cases simply having a break for 10 minutes, or, in serious or non-urgent situations, a few days, allows people to cool down and have a think. Quite often the group will feel differently after a bit of time out.

Since this is the easiest, and often the quickest, way of dealing with the situation, it's worth trying a break before going back to restart the discussion.

★ Go back to the stage about exploring people's needs and concerns. Use your active listening and questioning skills to help the person using the block to articulate themselves clearly, and to help the group to understand their concerns.

★ Ultimately if a group refuses to respect someone's block, then this may lead to that person leaving. It is important to remind everyone of that consequence.

Our group is biased towards the status quo

In any group there can be a resistance to change, with some people using the decision-making process to consistently stifle new initiatives and to maintain the status quo.

Many people are afraid of change and can feel challenged by new people wanting to introduce new ways of doing things. It can be hard to overcome this, but consensus should not be used to prevent innovation. Rather it can help to accommodate both the wish for change and the wish to protect that which is well-proved and working. If new ideas aren't being accepted then ultimately people will get frustrated and leave the group. At the same time it is well worth taking into account people's experience – there may be very good reasons why they are opposing something.

Some ideas to try:

★ A sub-group could go ahead with a project without everyone being involved.

★ A trial period for a new way of doing things, with a built in review process.

★ Identify what it is that people are afraid of and find solutions.

And finally...

The above suggestions for dealing with common problems that can crop up mainly offer only a quick or sticking plaster solution. It's worth considering the deeper challenges that we bring to our meetings, some of which we look at in Chapter 8: *Bridging the gap*.

Chapter 8:
Bridging the gap between theory and practice

It is easy to have a rosy vision of how consensus should work, and then feel disheartened when your day to day reality doesn't match up. We may say: "This is a way of making decisions based on the belief that we are all equally important," and "We're looking for win-win solutions that everyone is happy with," and it's good to remind each other what you are aiming for, but none of these things will come about just because you have said them. While Chapter 7: *Troubleshooting in your meetings* offers tips on things you can do in meetings when a problem arises, this chapter is about the more fundamental changes you can make in a group culture over the long term. We look at ways to respond to a range of more challenging situations, from making decisions when your options are constrained by external pressures; to tackling privilege and oppression and their effects on power dynamics; to addressing conflict; to open groups with fluctuating membership to scenarios where only a small minority of a group are really interested in consensus. Often these areas overlap – for example, the power dynamics in your group will affect the conflicts you have and how you deal with them; groups where the membership fluctuates may find it harder to deal with power imbalances.

A Consensus Handbook

Both conflict and power dynamics can stir up emotional and behavioural patterns that may have their roots in early childhood or in a lifetime's repeated experience of oppression. This chapter is not an alternative to months of therapy! We have tried not to over-simplify, or pretend things are easier that they are. However, we have focused on providing a better basic understanding of what is going on when our group dynamics are unhealthy. This chapter offers practical tips for groups that want to develop healthier dynamics, and get on with whatever kind of project they were set up for.

Conflict and consensus

People often associate conflict with arguments and bad feeling. However, another way of looking at it is that conflict simply involves people having values, needs or opinions that are, or seem to be, incompatible. We face conflict in every group or relationship we are in, although it can show itself in a variety of ways. Sometimes incompatibility can be straightforward to work around. At other times, conflict can bring up strong and uncomfortable feelings like anger and anxiety. It can often trigger emotions which have a longer history than the situation you are in. For example, someone whose childhood involved inconsistent parenting and repeatedly broken promises might have a much stronger reaction to changes of plan than someone whose early experiences were more secure. These responses can get in the way of the trust, respect and understanding we need to build consensus.

In everyday society we may have the option of turning to an outside authority when things get difficult, like complaining to the boss if a colleague is behaving in a way that we don't like. However, in many cases this doesn't actually solve the problem. Even if your boss takes you seriously, they are unlikely to be able to get to the root of the issue as effectively as you and your colleague could if you worked it out between yourselves. With greater understanding and skills we can find ways to deal with these situations ourselves. This section provides some pointers to help you with this in low level conflict situations. In more extreme cases you might want to get outside help of some kind.

Example of a conflict

Katy and Fahim are friends who have different ideas about how loud to play their music. Katy has been made homeless and comes to stay in Fahim's housing co-op. To begin with, Fahim is relaxed about Katy's music because he knows she needs somewhere to live, and it doesn't affect their relationship. But when she moves in longer term, loud music at funny hours of day and night stop him being able to sleep or relax. He starts to see the music as a sign that she has no respect for him. He becomes irritated by little things she does, like leaving dirty mugs lying about, and forgetting to clean her hair out of the plughole in the shower. She notices his tension and feels judged and unwelcome in the house. Initially, music, mugs and plughole are not mentioned, but they treat each other with frosty politeness.

Over time they become stuck in their narratives about the other person – Fahim believes that he is not respected, Katy that she is not welcome. Katy's response is to play the music even louder and leave her things in communal spaces to prove that it is her home too. In a house meeting she suggests a new system for storing recycling and Fahim argues strongly against any change to the way they've always done it. Finally, he trips over a bag that Katy has left in the middle of the floor and starts screaming at her in a way that is totally out of proportion to what, on the surface, has just happened.

The life cycle of a conflict

Incompatibility

In the example above we see how a simple difference becomes an incompatibility when it seems like both people can't get what they want at the same time – Katy can't have loud music at the same time as Fahim has silence in the house. Sometimes the incompatibility is harder to pin down, like having communication styles which don't work well together. For example, what one person thinks is playful banter may be taken by someone else as a crushing put down. In this case, neither person is getting what they want out of friendly interaction. Sometimes, it might only be one person who doesn't get their needs met, and others might not be aware of the conflict at all. Imagine one person in a group has strong ideas about how things should be done and always shares them with other people. If the rest of the group always follow these suggestions this first person may think everything is fine, and not realise that the others are growing increasingly resentful because they don't think it is acceptable to express opinions so strongly.

The effects on the relationship

The frustration that comes from unmet needs often leads to feelings, beliefs and behaviours which leak into the relationship. In our example above, we see how Katy's perception that she is unwelcome leads her into defiant behaviour that make the problem worse. Similarly, Fahim believes that he isn't respected, and comes to interpret everything she does as a confirmation of this. Sometimes the strength of our emotional response in a given situation may be a hangover from earlier experiences. For example, perhaps Katy came to the country where she now lives in her early teens and never quite felt welcomed. This makes her sensitive to similar dynamics replaying in adult life.

Frustration, and the beliefs and behaviours that people develop around it, can affect the ability to communicate with and accept the other person or group. Often tensions are expressed indirectly. For example, Katy and Fahim argue about how to store recycling, when the real issue was not what the waste paper bin should be used for, but who has ownership of the house, and the 'right' to come up with new ideas. Or it might be that people are no longer able to really listen to each other. If Fahim finally brought up the issue of the music after months of bad feeling, Katy might see it as an attack, and refuse to accept that he couldn't sleep with her bassline throbbing through the floorboards. For a different person the attitudes and behaviours might not be projected at the other person, but turned inwards. For example, someone else in Fahim's position might move from the belief that he wasn't respected by Katy to a belief that he wasn't worthy of respect by anyone. This could block communication by making it even harder for him to assert his own needs.

Ways of dealing with conflict

How often have you heard someone say, "I was really annoyed, but I didn't want to create conflict by making a fuss?" However, if we say that conflict is about your needs not being met because they seem to be incompatible with someone else's, then the conflict can't be *created* by making a fuss – it is already there, however you choose to respond. It is helpful to look at what our own usual responses are, and which responses are common in our group, in order to decide what we might want to do differently. Broadly speaking, these responses vary according to whether we are prioritising maintaining the relationship, meeting our own goals, both, or neither.

Accommodate: here you give up the thing you want for yourself, prioritising harmony in the relationship over your own needs and goals. For example, when Katy very first moves in, Fahim doesn't mention the music and remains relaxed and friendly with her. Choosing to accommodate to someone else's wishes could be a strategy for addressing power dynamics. In this example, perhaps Fahim makes an extra effort to let Katy do things her way in the house because he knows she is new and would otherwise be homeless. Or, in another group, you might actively support an idea you aren't that keen on, just because it was suggested by someone who rarely put ideas forward in meetings. If on the other hand, you are someone who always accommodates, you may end up feeling resentful or downtrodden.

Confront: if you are in confrontation then the priority is your own goals or needs, not the relationship. It is easy to characterise this response as 'selfish', but there are cases where it is appropriate. For example, if someone was picking on vulnerable members of your group you might not think much about maintaining the relationship when you challenged them. It is common for people to get stuck in confrontation over minor issues if they don't address the underlying problems. For example, Katy and Fahim have an underlying tension about who feels at home in the house, but it comes out through arguments about recycling.

Avoid: in this case you don't do anything for your goals *or* the relationship, like Fahim's behaviour when he continues to be silent about the music, but turns cold and distant with Katy. A common example in meetings is for contentious issues to never make it onto the agenda, or for someone to change the subject whenever difficult topics are brought up. Another pattern is for people to simply stop coming to groups when conflict arises, but never explain why.

Compromise: this goes part way to maintaining the relationship and to meeting the goals. Often it isn't based on a particularly deep analysis of the situation. For example, in the recycling conversation, Katy and Fahim might decide that they can each use their own system for storing recycling in the house, and take it out into the street themselves. With the music, they might decide that Katy turns the volume down by half. A compromise can often be worked out quite quickly if people are willing, and it maintains a relationship by showing a commitment to fairness. However, it is sometimes described as lose-lose because no-one quite gets what they want – the music is still too loud for Fahim and not loud enough for Katy. And coming to a settlement about what is done with the recycling doesn't get to the root of the disagreement.

Collaboration: is based on commitment to your own needs and goals, as well as to the relationship with the other person – in other words it works on the principles of consensus. It combines aspects of both confrontation and accommodation, and goes a step further than compromise, in that it takes a deeper understanding of what is going on to look for solutions which really work for everyone. Finding a way of effectively sound-proofing Katy's room might be a good collaborative solution to the initial music issue – that way she really could have noise at the same time as Fahim had silence. As well as

these kinds of practical solutions, the process of collaboration might involve an open conversation about what they each really needed, in this case in order to feel at home. This could lead to Katy finding more appropriate strategies for asserting ownership than leaving her things on the living room floor. Similarly, if Fahim felt less threatened, he might accept she had the right to new ideas about storing recycling.

Making choices about how to respond to conflict

Often the way we respond to conflict doesn't feel like a choice. Many of us are socially programmed to take a particular approach to conflict, regardless of whether it is appropriate for the situation. Some people learn early in life that confrontation is the only way to get their basic needs met. Others are expected to 'be good' and 'not cause trouble' and consistently accommodate. On top of this we need to deal with the other person's patterns – if their default setting is confrontation, then accommodation or avoidance might feel like the 'natural' response. However, becoming more aware of the different options open to us can help us start to make more conscious decisions about what approach to take in different situations.

We have prioritised collaboration in this chapter because this is the approach needed to reach synthesis – a fully supported consensus where everyone's needs are met. This is not going to be right for every situation – if someone attacks you in the street it may be *logically* possible to work with them to find a different way of getting money instead of taking yours, but self-preservation is likely to be your first priority. Collaboration takes trust, time and commitment, and people may only want to use this approach when both a relationship and our goals are important. Collaboration requires us to try to understand the other person's perspective even when we feel angry with them. It asks us to be honest with ourselves even when we feel vulnerable. There are lots of reasons why we might feel like we can't, or don't want to do this. In a situation in which you have been seriously hurt it might feel like too much. If the other person has a lot of power over you it might be more important to protect yourself. If they won't work with you, you can't collaborate on your own. On the other hand, collaboration has the potential to take you out of the conflict without either party needing to lose the thing you share – the group you are in. Through a deeper understanding of each person's needs it looks for a way to *remove* the incompatibility altogether, and carry on living, working or campaigning together. This might not always be possible, but the attempt will build a stronger relationship and a much better compromise than any quick fix or win-lose solutions.

Techniques for inviting collaboration

Create a supportive culture

The culture of interaction in a group makes a big difference to how easily people can bring up issues at an early stage, before frustrations have built up and affected the relationship. For example, you might have a regular slot in your meetings for giving feedback to each other, talking about how you are feeling about the group or for evaluating the meeting itself. A lot of groups set up mechanisms like this but rarely use them. However, if you regularly provide minor bits of feedback it will become a more normal part of your group culture and bringing up bigger issues may feel more possible.

Feedback is not just about things which don't work for you. Whether or not you use formal meeting slots to do it, giving each other positive recognition can help people feel valued. This may in turn mean that people are more able to handle conflict without losing

trust and understanding. This means taking the time to notice and tell someone when they do something well or put a lot of work into a task, including routine tasks which don't usually come with much prestige. Some people will appreciate it if you ask about what is going on in their life outside the group, so long as you remember what they said last time – asking the same question five times probably won't help them feel listened to! This doesn't mean you have to all be friends with each other, or even like each other. Finding out what you can respect and appreciate in each person, and making efforts to at least understand the rest, will help you make effective decisions together.

Giving positive recognition doesn't mean you have to gloss over things you don't like. If you feel you are in a group where disagreements aren't voiced, and frustrations are suppressed, see what you can do to respectfully bring them to the surface. For example, if a decision appears to be going ahead with only a few enthusiastic voices behind it, be proactive about asking for anyone who has concerns. If, outside of meetings, people regularly complain about the group as a whole or individuals within it, encourage them to bring it up. If you sense tensions or bad atmosphere, try to deal with it directly.

Simple facilitation techniques can reduce the chances of conflict damaging your group. For example, it is common for people to go away with different interpretations of a discussion, and then to lose trust when other people don't do what they expected. Instead, agree the exact wording of a decision and write it down at the time that it is made. This could include going into more detail. Perhaps you are a worker's co-op developing a sick pay policy. It could be a good idea to hear from each person to check you have a similar understanding of 'too ill to work' or else resentment could build up when someone stays off with a slight cold. In a group where trust is already low, check through and agree the minutes at the end of a meeting while everyone's memory is fresh and there is still time to change things. During a meeting, techniques like active listening and summarising can help to identify any misunderstandings, and bring them into the open before too much tension has grown up around them.

Being honest about what you really need

Collaboration means we may give up some of what we *want*, but it aims to give us all of what we really *need*. Differentiating between wants and needs isn't always easy in practice. Returning to the housing co-op example above, clearly Katy didn't *need* to play music at home in the sense that it was necessary for her survival. The same could be said for Fahim wanting silence. However, they clearly both felt these things were very important in order for them to feel at home. Other things they did may also have been strategies to feel more at home, even if they didn't think that through consciously, such as Katy leaving her things in communal areas, and Fahim resisting any changes to the recycling system. However, these strategies may not have been *necessary* in order for them to feel at home. As we suggested above, collaboration might involve both of them finding new ones that enabled them to share ownership of the house.

Before you can get to the stage of having these conversations with someone else, it helps if you can be honest with yourself about what you want and why. This isn't always easy. For example, we have been assuming that Fahim's resistance to Katy's new recycling idea was that on some level he believed that her feeling ownership of the house threatened his right to feel it too. However, admitting this would mean admitting ungenerous feelings, so he may have found it more convenient to think he was so annoyed by her suggestion because it made the house look messy, even if none of their other housemates seemed to think so.

Being honest might also mean accepting that you have been wanting someone to meet a need that wasn't really their responsibility. For example, maybe you have spent months feeling frustrated because you have joined a climate action group where no-one else seems to see the value of having fun together outside of meetings. You may have supplied hundreds of very good reasons why socialising outside meetings is good for group dynamics, and still everyone insists that they don't really have time. Thinking hard about why it is so important to you may reveal that maintaining relationships in the group isn't your only priority – actually you are looking for people to go out dancing with, and you spend so much time on your activism that the people you see in meetings are the easiest ones to ask. If it's not something they want to do, claiming it is for the sake of group dynamics may be doubly counter-productive – it may be bad for dynamics, and prevent them from seeing that you actually want their friendship for its own sake.

Thinking about what other people might need

Some people spend a lot of time guessing what is really going on for other people. At best, this can help us be ready to empathise, and find ways forward. For example, someone suggests something which most people in the group like, but one person passionately insists it is impractical and a waste of time. If they actually oppose the idea for more personal reasons they'd rather not express, then taking them at face values and debating the practicalities could leave you talking in circles for a very long time. Instead, offering them respect and recognition could bolster their trust in you, so they became more able to discuss the real issues.

However, when we start second guessing other people, and then finding ways to work round the problem, there is a danger we could be manipulating them. After all, it can be tempting to search out someone's underlying emotional needs when you don't want to listen to the content of what they are saying. Maybe the idea you like *is* quite impractical, and it is you who doesn't want to admit it. For this reason your first question needs to be "What is actually going on for *me*?" Rather than trying to mind-read, a better approach is to use open questions to encourage other people to be honest with themselves as well. For example: "Everyone has made practical arguments for what they think we should do but we don't seem to be moving towards agreement on anything. I wonder how everyone is *feeling* about the ideas?" Or simply, "There seems to be a lot of tension in the room. I'd be interested to hear if anyone has anything they're holding back from saying?"

If you know someone well enough, you might want to tell them what you guess is going on for them, but be very clear that you know it is a guess, and be open to being told you are wrong: "You seem to have lots of reasons why Jemma's idea won't work, but I don't really agree that it would be as difficult as you think. My interpretation of this situation is that you have another anxiety going on. For example that you'll end up with an unfair share of the workload if we put it into practice?" This is a tactic best used with caution, because some people will feel annoyed, or think it patronising. Another approach when you think someone else has something they aren't saying, is to think hard about whether they have been getting the basic respect they deserve, and then trying to put back anything that might be missing. For example, listen carefully to the things that they say, give them recognition for the things they have done for the group, and if you think it might help, encourage them to open up about where their tension might come from.

Setting up a conversation about the conflict

Often in consensus groups conflict will emerge in meetings. You might need to deal with it straight away, for instance because you have an urgent decision to make. However, communication about underlying issues often goes better if everyone concerned has a bit more time to think about it. If it is possible, take a break from a meeting where you are struggling to reach agreement – people may well return with a clearer idea of what they want and a better capacity to listen. On the flip side, there is the danger that if people have a preference for avoiding conflict they may not return. If it is important to have the conversation with that particular group of people you might want to keep the break short, or get a clear commitment from everybody to come to the next meeting.

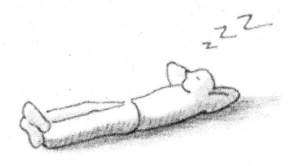

Another issue is whether a meeting is the right setting to have the conversation at all. On the one hand, if a number of people are affected by something then they might want to be involved in talking about it. If there is an issue you are anxious about bringing up with somebody, you might feel more secure knowing there will be other people there who share your perspective. For example, if someone shouted at you in a meeting in a way you found abusive you might not feel particularly safe talking to them about it one on one. On the other hand, some people find honesty easier if fewer people are present. The person who shouted at you might be more ready to apologise if it doesn't mean losing face in front of a roomful of people. If one person has difficult relationships with a number of people in the group, then it might sometimes be better to have several one-on-one conversations than to try to get everyone together and sort it all out at once.

Remember, even if it is you who is raising an issue, the decisions about when and where to have the conversation, and who else should be there, are not just yours. It is best to give the person or people you want to speak to a broad outline of what you want to talk about and then decide other details with them. This might be as simple as saying, for example, "I'd like to chat about the noise levels in the house, when would be a good time?" Or it might involve more complicated logistics around neutral venues, and who is prepared to be in the same room together. If you are planning to talk about the issue in a meeting, it could help to mention it to individuals in person, before it goes out as an agenda item. Think about your wording and how people might respond to it. For example, people might arrive with more open minds to a meeting about "distribution of tasks" than to one about "some people not doing their fair share"!

The tips below on ways of expressing yourselves can be applied in meetings or one on one situations. Generally, preparation will help you work out what you want to say and how, but the basic principles can be applied at any point you are in a conflict situation.

A Consensus Handbook

Expressing what you feel

If we can honestly express our thoughts and feelings, other people may find it much easier to empathise with us. This may help them see beyond any assumptions about us, and our behaviour in the conflict. It also paves the way for a discussion of their needs as well as ours.

Showing and talking about feelings

Your preferred way of bringing something up will depend a lot on your own culture and habits. You might also want to think about who you are talking to and what they are able to hear. Some people find it much easier to connect to and understand an emotion if you *show* it to them instead of just talking about it – if you shout at them or burst into tears it will help them recognise something is important to you. Other people may be uncomfortable around displays of anger or distress, possibly seeing it as manipulative, and find it much easier to hear what you are saying when you are more calm. You might not feel you have much choice about how you express yourself, or you might not want to adapt it to suit other people. For example, in northern Europe, the stereotypes are for middle-class cultures to avoid showing anger, and masculine cultures to hide vulnerability. You might well argue that these cultures are dominant enough, and there is no reason for you to fit their norms simply in order to be taken seriously. However, communication can be more effective if you are aware of the preferences of the person or people on the receiving end as well as your own. If you feel you aren't getting through to some people with your feelings on display, then a pragmatic decision might be to explain yourself a second time after you've calmed down.

Naming your feelings without blaming anyone

Being honest about what you feel shows self-respect, you aren't pretending your feelings are something else in order to be taken seriously. It can also help other people to empathise with you and to be honest in their turn. It can help to talk about feelings in a way that doesn't imply they are anyone's fault – our own, or someone else's. This is a bit counter-intuitive if you have been brought up in a culture where blame is very normal, so here is a detailed explanation.

Returning to the housing co-op example, consider Fahim's anger with Katy's music. This anger certainly isn't *his* fault – he wants to relax and the music is preventing him. Feelings like irritation, anger or disappointment shouldn't be suppressed. Nor does it help anyone if we turn those feelings inward – deciding we are a bad person for feeling angry, 'pathetic' for feeling hurt, etc. However, Katy didn't *make* him feel angry, any more than the sea can *make* you drown. His anger comes from the fact that *his* needs aren't being met – none of the other housemates particularly need silence and they aren't bothered by the music.

People usually do things to meet their own needs, and very rarely have the *intention* that we should respond in a particular way. The main point here is that even when you have strong feelings, the answer isn't *necessarily* that the other person should change the behaviour that triggered those feelings. It might mean you making changes yourself, or accepting that their behaviour doesn't mean what you think it does. For example, maybe you get upset if someone ignores you when they are working. You might want to demand they pay you more attention, or simply write them off as cold or rude. However, part of the answer may simply be for you to recognise that this is about their need to concentrate, not about them not liking you. This doesn't mean that they shouldn't *consider* your feelings. For example, if they know that you find it hard to be in the same group as someone who doesn't acknowledge you for long periods of time, they could learn to give you a nice smile before asking you to let them finish. Nor do you have to give up what you really need. For as long as you want to go on sharing something – a house, or a relationship or a group – you all have a responsibility to find ways of meeting your needs that don't get in the way of anyone else's. Giving other people information about how you feel is the first step in a collaborative process which takes into account everyone's feelings.

'I statements'

A formula for expressing feelings without blame is known as the 'I statement': *When you (+ behaviour), I...* For example, "When you play your music so loud, I can't sleep." "When the meeting starts late, I get frustrated." "When we make a plan and then you don't turn up, I stop wanting to make any more plans with you." In this way you can name the two things – the other person's behaviour and your response, without implying that the one is the direct and only cause of the other, (as in "You make me angry", or "I'm angry because you..."). Keeping your account of the behaviour as fact-based as possible can help pinpoint exactly what bothers you. For example, "You often leave your things in the living room" may be more helpful than "You're lazy and messy". Using the 'I statement' formula may have the added benefit of the other people becoming less defensive. However, if you express yourself in this way simply in order to get a better response from them they may detect it and feel manipulated – as always, honesty is key.

For example, be aware of whether what you say about your own feelings is an indirect comment on the other person's or people's behaviour. You might say "I *feel* exploited/ignored/betrayed/let down" but in fact these words are not so much about how you feel as how you *interpret* someone else's behaviour. These interpretations may be an important part of why you feel what you do, and you might have good reason to want to present them to the other people. However, *if* you want to stick to the 'I statement' formula, then "I feel overworked/lonely/disappointed/frustrated" talks purely about what is going on for you. A test is whether someone could deny what you said. For example, if someone says "I feel frozen out of the group", it is easy to respond with "We're not freezing you out", whereas "I feel alone in this group" is much harder to glibly contradict. This can reduce the potential for the other person to respond defensively.

On the other hand, you might find this dishonest. For example, you could translate "I feel betrayed" to "I feel disappointed", but it wouldn't really do justice to how complex your feelings are. Plus, explaining how you interpret someone's behaviour could help them understand why you feel so strongly about it. "I always do the cleaning and I feel angry about it, because I think you are exploiting me." You might need to get this interpretation off your chest in order to listen to their view on the matter, "I don't see it as exploitation, I just don't think it is necessary to hoover the carpet every day." This doesn't mean you have to agree – simply recognise their different perspective.

There is no single right answer as to whether it is helpful to let other people know how you judge their behaviour, but it does help to be aware that it can produce a strong reaction. Use phrases like "I think...", "My interpretation of that is...", "In my head, that means..." to acknowledge that they might see it differently.

Where to go from there

If you have spent a long time preparing what you want to say, it is easy to forget that collaboration also involves drawing out the other person's perspective, which is harder to plan for! Broadly speaking, the aim is to come to an understanding of each other's needs and perspectives on the situation as it stands, and work from there to find new ways forward. This can be easier if you accept from the outset that the other person will have a different memory and interpretation of whatever has happened in the past. For example, a protracted back and forth about whether someone really said the words that you found so hurtful, may undermine goodwill and not take you forward. If you can tell someone "What I *remember* you saying is... and what I *believe* you meant by it was..." they might be able to accept your feelings, even if they still insist that what they intended to say was something different.

If you have led the way with honesty and feel like they are covering up what they really think and feel, or are refusing to accept your thoughts and feelings, you may well feel angry with them. However, be aware that defensiveness is often a stage that people pass through. You can tell them you don't think they are really listening to you, and ask them to meet you again when they have had a bit of time to think. These kinds of delays may be frustrating, but they can be a better option than wrangling over details. You've had time to consider things, they probably need it too! Also watch out for someone who goes to the opposite extreme and seems to agree with and accept everything you have said about their behaviour. They may have decided that being accommodating to your version of events is the easiest way to avoid having to really talk about it. Or they too may need to process what you have said in order to 'discover' their own point of view before attempting a constructive dialogue about what to do next. However careful you were to express your feelings without blame, they may still believe that it is there, and blame themselves too.

Get yourself ready to listen, even if you don't like what you hear. Be aware that if you have spent your time rehearsing 'I statements' what you get back from other people may come in less carefully chosen words. For example, if they say "You make me feel inadequate", remember that this is a very common turn of phrase, and it doesn't necessarily indicate that they think the feeling is your fault. Rather than becoming defensive yourself, or insisting they express themselves in the way you consider to be correct before you will listen, try to pick out the information that will help you move forwards – their feelings, and the behaviours of yours that trigger it.

Try to show an interest in their perspective without losing sight of your own. For example, maybe you work with someone who consistently arrives late in the mornings. You can show understanding for why they find it hard to get their kids ready and arrive in work at the agreed time, but still insist that you want their help with the early morning jobs. Or perhaps someone tells you that they find you cold and distant. It is fine to tell them that you haven't been very outgoing recently because you are suffering from depression. However, it helps if you can also accept that they perceive you in a particular way, regardless of whether you think this perception is 'fair.'

Remember as well that in order to get everything you really need, you may well have to give up some of the things you want. If the issue is arriving late to work, then perhaps your colleague really can't come in on time. In this case you need to think about whether you really need everyone there first thing in the morning, in which case the only solution might be to find

someone else to join your worker's co-op. Alternatively, maybe what you need is to feel the work is distributed fairly, and if they take on all the jobs at the end of the day so you can leave early it might be OK. Be aware also, that none of these options are likely to feel as comfortable to them as carrying on as things are, so don't be surprised if they are reluctant to acknowledge the problem at first. Stick at it – if you cannot carry on working there as things are then they have a responsibility to help find another way round the problem.

Whatever solutions you come to, it can help take the pressure off if you think you are just trying them out. You might not be convinced by the idea of your colleague taking on end of the day jobs instead, but you could still try it out for a limited time period, with a commitment to review how it is going after a fixed time. It can make it easier to let go of things you want if you know you both have the option of revisiting the decision, and if you are deeply unhappy you can say so at any point.

The final option is to decide whether the incompatibility is so fundamental that you cannot go on sharing whatever it is you share, or whether it is better to reach a compromise, however unsatisfactory, than to split. If you are part of a campaign group that has long running disagreements about who they should be targeting, there maybe a very limited range of actions you can do together, and you might get more done as two groups. By contrast, a residents' association in a block of flats might be able to divide into different working groups so that certain people didn't have to spend too much time together, but they might undermine each other if they split entirely and started putting opposing demands to the landlord, or one group started laying tarmac where the other was planning to dig flower beds. Even in situations where you opt for a split, the attempt to collaborate for a good solution can help everyone feel they have had a fair deal in the division, and enable you to work together on specific things in future.

Power dynamics

Sadly, we can't get from today's unjust society to one where everyone is equal simply by saying that is where we want to be. The reality is that in any group, even one which uses consensus and is committed to non-hierarchy, some people will be feeling more empowered and comfortable than others. Who this is might vary from situation to situation, but particularly when it is the same people a lot of the time, these characters can end up dominating the group. The reason for this might be that they've been heavily involved for a long time, or that they have grown up with privileges that mean they are more used to the idea that their needs are valid and their ways of doing things are OK.

The problem here is *not* the fact that they feel empowered and comfortable. If everyone felt their needs were valid and their way of doing things was OK, and the power to do things in the group was shared between everybody it would be great. The difficulty arises when there are big imbalances between members of the group, or some people use their power against others. For example, someone who is very involved might see themselves as indispensable, and insist that meeting times are always fitted around their personal timetable, even if that means that there are other people who can never make it. Or it might simply always be the same people who express their views and feelings when an issue is discussed, meaning that ultimately the decisions always go their way. If this is the case then a group is not really using consensus, because it will not be finding solutions which work for the people who are less able to express their views.

Step one: What are our feelings about power dynamics?

Realising our group is not as non-hierarchical as it claims to be can be dispiriting, and can stir up feelings of guilt, shame and anger. This can particularly be the case when the root of the problem is in social inequalities that impact on the whole of people's lives – not just their interactions in this particular group. People can respond to guilt, shame and anger in a number of ways. These feelings can provide the impetus for change. Alternatively, people can be paralysed by these feelings to the extent that they don't feel able to look honestly at their behaviour and work out how to change it so they take more, or less, power in a situation.

An approach that some people find helpful to avoid paralysis is to recognise that these feelings are valid, but also to recognise that the behaviours that triggered those feelings are part of a system of oppression and exploitation that has a much longer history than their particular group and the individuals within it. This approach acknowledges that we all have responsibility to learn to behave in ways that are more equal (and therefore it's understandable to feel angry or guilty if we, or someone else, is not doing that). At the same time, it accepts that this learning process takes time for everyone, and if we haven't got to where we want to be yet, it doesn't make us 'bad' people.

For example, imagine someone in your group makes a casually snobby comment. They may be a product of the class system, and they are certainly perpetuating it, but they didn't technically create the whole structure of social and economic exploitation. On the other hand, it is understandable if sometimes they get the full brunt of your rage as if they did. After all, consensus decision making is all about human equality, and it can be very disappointing when people don't live out the politics they believe in. Plus, it is very common to internalise oppression – to believe, emotionally, if not rationally, that there is something wrong with you if you haven't got a fair deal in life. Discovering anger at the outside world can be an important stage in undoing that internalised oppression, and it is not surprising if that anger is sometimes directed disproportionately at the people

A Consensus Handbook

around you. However, remember that the behaviour that triggered your anger, resentment or shame may well come from the other person's insecurity, or at least their lack of awareness, and is unlikely to be about them being deliberately malicious. For example, maybe you feel intimidated by someone who takes up a lot of space talking in large meetings, but perhaps they do it to make up for their own feelings of inadequacy in more informal social situations.

Similarly, if someone directs that kind of anger at you, or even gently challenges you on something you have said or done, remembering the wider perspective can help you put guilt and defensiveness to one side. If you are a white person and someone calls you racist, for example, a common response might be to feel like a terrible person and shut down, or to deny it altogether. A healthier way of dealing with it might be to use what was said to become more aware of the privileges you have benefited from, or how your behaviour impacts on other people. You can do this even if you don't immediately agree with their interpretation of the situation. For example, maybe you and your group have travelled to another city for a demonstration and you get lost at night in a neighbourhood that your guidebook describes as 'rough'. Afterwards, someone points out that you chose the only white person in the street to ask directions from. You may think that the reason that you felt safer approaching this person was that they were also the only one you identified as a woman, and believe that this was a more acceptable reason to trust them than the colour of their skin. However, it shows more respect to the person who challenged you, and greater honesty with yourself, if you also seriously consider their suggestion that, at a sub-conscious level, race may also have played a part in your decision.

Along with anger and guilt, another common dynamic is for people to develop a competitive attitude around different forms of privilege. A classic example would be a middle class woman and a working class man debating whether patriarchy or the class system is 'the real problem', as if there wasn't enough oppression to go round, and acknowledging someone else's might cancel out their own share. If you find you are feeling resentful when someone complains they have been abused, exploited or overlooked, it is worth stepping back and thinking about where that feeling comes from. Maybe you have things of your own to complain about, and feel these could be given more attention. Sometimes you might want to do this by bringing your own experiences into the conversation, at other times you can simply acknowledge them to yourself. Either way, this can be done alongside a recognition that other people may have experienced a similar dynamic for different reasons, and there may be situations where you have unfair advantages, as well as others where you are disadvantaged.

One final feeling to consider is hope. It is easy to lose motivation if progress is slower than you expected. Challenging these patterns can be more difficult than organising an event or an action or setting up a new project. It means going against years of our own socialisation in a divided and competitive society. It means changing our feelings and beliefs about ourselves and other people. And however much honesty and understanding you achieve, you will still face defensiveness from other people, and recognise it occasionally in yourself. Whatever you do to learn to live and work as equals, there will still be times when you don't take the power that is due to you, or you exert power over others. Don't give up, sorting out your power dynamics is an important part of making consensus decisions real, and whatever steps you take to a more equal and balanced dynamic deserve pride and recognition.

Step two: Diagnosis – what is actually going on in your group?

We often have a strong sense for what the power dynamics in a group are, but it can help to also work out what is going on in a more objective way. For example, you might particularly notice the dominant behaviour of someone you find socially irritating, and overlook it in someone you are friends with. Looking at how important decisions are made in your group may help you assess how balanced your power dynamics are. These decisions may be taken on a day to day basis, but they shape the direction of your group over time. Examples of these decisions are: What things should you prioritise doing? How should you use your resources?

Questions to ask yourselves

★ **How are decisions made?** Do they go to meetings or are there key people in your group who decide what needs doing and then just get on with it? If someone has a question about whether to do something, are there particular people who they are more likely to ask, and then take their opinion as permission? Or do you make enough clear policy decisions and share enough information in meetings that everyone is equally able to make judgement calls for themselves, or work out whether they need to check in with everyone? For example, in a workers' co-op, one person might agree to work that came in without checking what anyone else thought, while others put it to a meeting. Neither of these options is intrinsically better – whether it is useful to check with the whole co-op first will depend on the circumstances – the key question is whether everyone is doing the same.

★ If these decisions are made in meetings, **who participates?** Is everyone equally involved? Or are there some people who don't go, or don't get involved in the discussion as much? When people speak, are they all equally likely to be listened to (which isn't the same as agreed with)? And when people talk, what are they talking about? There is a world of difference between opening your mouth to say "Does anyone want a cup of tea?" or even "I think the text on the leaflet should be bigger" and having the openness and trust to assert more 'difficult' needs, like "I think that action is too risky" or "I really don't want that person to join our band."

★ And **how are decisions implemented?** Are there some people who do what they want and ignore or forget what was agreed? When people take on tasks, are there some who don't get any guidance at all from the group, while for others every detail is micro-managed?

Exactly how people participate in a group will vary over time. People will take on different roles depending on personal things like day to day fluctuations in their mental and physical health as well as the context, like what topic is being discussed, or what tasks are taken on. Sometimes a power dynamic will right itself quickly. For example, someone who is quite confident might be briefly intimidated by someone else's expertise, and then realise their own contributions are equally valid, even if they can't express them in the same technical terms. The key, therefore, is to look for repeat patterns across several meetings, so you can identify where the more entrenched problems lie.

Step three: Where do your power imbalances come from?

Identifying what patterns there are in your group is important, but to change them, it helps to think about where they came from. The answer to this will rarely be simple. For example, Fred might not speak very often in meetings, and an immediate reason for this might be that the group isn't sharing enough information early on in the discussion for him to understand the issues that are being talked about. However, there might be a longer term problem: if Fred had more confidence and self-trust he might ask about the things he didn't understand instead of sitting in silence. And if the rest of the group valued him more highly, they might notice he wasn't talking, and fill him in on the details he was missing. In this example, people could make the situation a little better by spending more time introducing the issue, as suggested in the consensus process outlined in Chapter 1: *Making decisions by consensus*. However, if there is an underlying power dynamic in which Fred is consistently undervalued both by himself and the rest of the group, sharing information in a meeting is unlikely to go far enough to change things.

Who's most involved?

In this example, it may be that Fred's silence is linked to the fact that most of the talking in the meetings is done by a small group of people who are heavily involved. These people may have got into

A Consensus Handbook

this position of power through commitment to the project, rather than a desire to dominate. They may talk more because they have a greater overview of what needs doing, care more what decisions are made and are better informed about the options. Other people may defer to them because they always know where things are kept, how things work and what happened last time an idea was tried out. In this case, steps need to be taken to make it easier for people to get involved in the things the group does, not just to make it easier for them to talk in meetings. A key thing to remember is that we are looking for ways to share power, not simply to take it away from the people who have it. The answer is not to resent and ignore the people who have more experience, but for people who are new to build up their involvement, so they gain the knowledge and understanding to take shared responsibility for making good decisions.

Who does what?

Are there some people who always take on tasks that society considers high status, and other people are very involved, but always do jobs that are considered 'menial'? It can often be the case that the people who do more respected jobs are also treated like more important people. For example, if one person always makes the leaflets and someone else 'only' delivers them they may not participate as equals in meetings. In some direct action groups, it is common for people who take part in actions to get seen as somehow more important than the people who drive them there, or cook food before they set off, or go along to court to cheer them on. There can be a similar dynamic around jobs that are traditionally gendered. For example, if you live on a protest site, cooking, constructing defences against eviction, chopping wood and washing up are all equally necessary jobs, and all require learnt skills. However, it is not unusual to find that there is a gender divide in who does those jobs, and for the people with the skills that are considered masculine also to be accorded a higher status.

Who feels at home?

Another dynamic is around what 'kind' of people feel at home in the group. Consensus provides a radically alternative way to make decisions, compared to direct voting, representative democracy or straightforward hierarchy. People who choose to join consensus groups are often 'alternative' in other ways too: they may be anarchists, feminists and environmentalists; they might work in co-ops, or devote their spare time to campaigning against something they see as unfair. They often go through life feeling like they are in some way different from mainstream society. It is common for those people to forget that in the 'alternative' groups in which they get the rare pleasure of feeling 'normal', there is usually someone else who is feeling like a misfit and an outsider. They may feel isolated partly because of a lack of self-confidence, rather than because the people who are on the 'inside' of the group actively exclude them. For example, if Fred generally isn't very comfortable in himself, he may dislike being in a group where everyone dresses differently to him, even if he is welcomed with open minds and arms. However, it is common for people who feel at home in a group to do and say things which contribute to others feeling marginalised. For example, maybe the group are slower to trust Fred with secret details about planned actions than someone else who looked more similar to them.

A Consensus Handbook

Social privileges

It is not just 'alternative' people who get to feel at home in consensus groups. In fact, the internal power dynamics of consensus groups are often much closer to those of wider society than people like to admit. Sometimes this is explicit, like people making sexist jokes or assuming a disabled person is helpless and needs everything doing for them. Sometimes, it is harder to spot the connections between your group dynamics and wider social ones. For example it may always be the same people taking on organisational roles. You might assume that this is because they have more time to be involved, but it is worth questioning whether they all come from a similar background. For example, middle class people are often brought up with the expectation that they will do 'professional' jobs, and are more likely to be confident about their abilities in a 'managerial' role. Sometimes social privilege is more about what is *not* said or done, e.g. does your group take a month's break each year while 'everyone' goes to see family for Christmas and this is the only festival which is ever mentioned? Do people make sweeping statements about men and women, and seem to forget that there are people who don't want to or can't fit either category? Do your meetings happen up at the top of a five storey building with no lift, and no-one thinks about people who can't climb stairs because they're never there to point out their exclusion? Do posters for the group's events get put up in the wholefood shop, the arthouse cinema and the university but not the laundrettes, the chippy and the bingo hall? The assumptions, about who 'we' are, behind these examples can have an impact that is greater than the sum of their parts. If your life experiences or culture are never acknowledged, then it is likely to undermine your sense of belonging to the group and your ability to find the trust and openness needed for consensus. And, of course, if you are never able to be there at all, because the publicity is never aimed at you, or because the group chooses an inaccessible venue, then you will be even further from being 'at home' in a group.

Recognising the role of privilege and oppression in how people behave is not so simple as assuming that dominant people are privileged and quieter ones are oppressed. For example, some people might respond to their own oppression with a strong need for achievement to prove themselves. This may come out as a desire to plan everything thoroughly, and do everything well. If other people have the same desire, there may be resulting tussles over what 'well' means, but the power dynamics can still be fairly equal. On the other hand, people with a more relaxed attitude may experience this behaviour as controlling. Or there may be some people in the group whose frustrations are often expressed as anger. If other group members find this intimidating, then the angry people may always get their way. On the other hand, they may find their views are disregarded because their anger is not seen as socially acceptable. In other words, oppression shows itself in complicated ways, and the assumptions we make about how other people have 'had it easy' are often inaccurate.

Step four: Work out some ways to change your power dynamics

We have assembled a few tips and thoughts below about things you can do to balance out the power dynamics in your group. It is by no means a comprehensive list. Hopefully, these ideas will spark off more of your own – try them out, refine them and share them – equalising power dynamics is work in progress for all of us. Some of these ideas are concrete suggestions – for example a series of questions to ask about a venue to consider different aspects of accessibility. Others are more about the approach that you take and can be applied in a number of situations, like encouraging your group to take shared responsibility for tackling poor dynamics.

Shared responsibility

Because some people react defensively when you point out their role in power imbalances it can be tempting to try to deal with them on your own. For example, you might realise you are doing a lot of the talking and decide to hold back. If the gap you leave is filled by other people who were already speaking a lot you may end up feeling self-righteous and resentful without having changed anything. Being more open might make it easier for the group to share responsibility for the change. For example, you could say: "I've noticed we're all doing very different amounts of speaking. Personally, I've decided to

A Consensus Handbook

try and hold back a bit, but I wonder if anyone else feels it is a problem and would like to suggest anything else we could do differently." Or, if it's someone else's position of power you want to challenge: "I've noticed that Sam has the greatest overview of the finances, and I've caught myself asking her what we can afford instead of bringing my questions to a meeting. That doesn't feel like a very fair on Sam or the rest of you, because she's going to end up making decisions about what's worth spending money on. Can we have a finances skillshare so we're not giving all that power and responsibility to Sam?"

Offering each other support makes a massive difference when challenging power dynamics. It is a common scenario for strong characters to keep each other in check, while everyone else keeps their head down and avoids getting mixed up in conflict. For example, perhaps someone is insisting on their favourite plan, even though it clearly won't work for other people. If another person challenges them, it is easy to keep quiet yourself. However, this puts pressure on people who are already dominant to stay in that role in order to balance out other dominant people. There is a much better chance of really changing the situation if a range of people in the group take responsibility for challenging abuses of power. The conflict section above has ideas on how to raise these issues.

Take it a step at a time

Another general principle is that deeply ingrained power dynamics are unlikely to change overnight, and achieving change may take patience. Sudden breakthroughs may be followed by unexpected setbacks, but this isn't a reason to give up. It is easy to have a moment of self-realisation, ("Aagh! I keep my mouth shut til I've heard what Rakesh has to say, and then I go along with that,") and then find that you are doing exactly the same next meeting – the only difference being that you notice afterwards and get cross with yourself. Follow up your moments of insight with small achievable changes in behaviour ("Next time I catch myself doing it, I'll stop and think hard about whether I really believe in what I've just said and if I don't, I'll say I've changed my mind.") Similarly, the dynamics of the whole group aren't going to shift instantly just because you have named them. Try to recognise steps forward for what they are, and keep pushing for more.

Is your group accessible to as many people as possible?

The first and most basic step to challenging power dynamics in a group is to make sure that everyone who wants to be part of it can come to your meetings and events. This doesn't mean that an anti-fascist group needs to welcome members of a racist political party. Nor does it mean that it is always wrong to get together with a few friends and get on with doing something without including anyone else. However, if you do want an open group, then make sure you don't exclude people who would otherwise agree with your aims.

It's up to people already in a group to be pro-active about this, because the people who are left out may never provide feedback. We've already provided the example of the group that meets up five flights of stairs – someone who can't get there at all may not put lots of effort into pointing out how exclusive this is – it's up to people in the group to work it out. Similarly, if you do all your publicity on social media sites them someone who uses email (or the postal service!) is unlikely to ask you to do it in any other way because they won't know you exist. The following tips will make it easier for people to find out about, and get to your meetings.

Publicity

The first question is who knows the event is happening. Think about where your publicity goes. Try talking to people who are involved in groups with very different memberships about what they find the most effective ways of publicising an event. This might be as simple as finding out where there are noticeboards in parts of town you don't usually go to. Alternatively, it may involve things like getting your leaflets translated, or printing some in larger text.

The second question is about who can get there. There isn't always a perfect venue, (although there are tips below on finding the best you can). Gather accurate information about the venue and the event and list all access features clearly in all your publicity, e.g.:

★ 2 parking spaces for blue badge holders;

★ level entrance to the building from the car park;

★ stepped entrance with a handrail on the left;

★ hearing induction loop in the meeting room;

★ vegetarian, vegan, halal and kosher food available;

★ baby-changing facilities and crèche available.

Giving this level of detail will not only help someone decide whether to come. It also helps them trust that access has been thought about in advance, so they are more likely to get in touch with questions or feedback.

Choosing a venue to hire

Sometimes the only venue you can afford is someone's front room, and even when you are paying, the choices can be limited. The following list of questions will help you pick and make the best of what is available. Ask and listen to feedback about how accessible your event is so you can extend this list for next time.

To find out about venues with disabled access, you could contact your local disability rights organisation – look in the Yellow Pages or Phone Book (under "Disabled – Information and Services") or ask your local council or Citizen's Advice Bureau for contact information.

Visit the venue before booking it to check accessibility. Here are some things to check:

★ What are the public transport links? Are any of these accessible, if so in what ways?

★ Is there a car park or any area near the front door for cars? If so, are there marked blue badge spaces? If not, consider reserving the parking spaces for badge holders.

★ Is the 'accessible entrance' kept locked? If so, this is sending a clear message to wheelchair users and people with mobility impairments that they are not wanted. Insist that the locked entrance is kept unlocked for the duration of your time in the building. Make sure that the path up to the accessible entrance is not blocked by wheelie bins, rubbish bags, advertising boards etc.

★ Is the adapted toilet kept locked? If so, make sure that it is unlocked while you are in the building. Non-disabled adults do not have to ask for permission to use the toilet, so why should disabled people? Is the adapted toilet clean and free of clutter?

★ Is there a loop system in your meeting room for hearing aid users? If so, is it working? Does anyone know how to switch it on or alter the volume? If so, will that person be there when you hold your event in the building?

★ Are there clear signposts from the entrance to the room?

★ Are there any visual flashing fire alarms in the toilets to alert deaf and hearing impaired people of fire? If not, consider what you will need to do in an emergency.

★ Is the baby changing area accessible to disabled people?

★ Is the venue child-friendly? Are there obvious hazards, such as unlocked doors that open onto busy roads, or stairs with no stair gates.

★ Does the venue have a private room that can be used as prayer spaces? Remember some faiths require followers to pray at regular intervals. Does your event timetable allow for this?

★ Finally, if anyone complains about access to your venue, listen carefully and make a note of the difficulties so that you can either sort out the problem or add the information to future publicity.

Creating a group where more people can feel at home

Making sure that people can get to your meetings is just the starting point. Creating a culture in which a diverse range of people feels relaxed and able to take ownership and initiative requires time and work. Unfortunately, there is no simple checklist to follow here, although there are a few things you can do at events that avoid excluding people in really obvious ways. For example, you can adapt handouts for visually impaired people, book sign language interpreters and translators, and make sure any food you provide caters for all diets.

To deal with more subtle forms of exclusion, there is a strong case for building up your self-awareness, pausing to reflect on how the little things you say and do give messages about who 'we' are. This applies to everyone – even if you feel on the outside of the group or mainstream society a lot of the time, there will be some ways in which you leave other people out. However, it is particularly important if you are someone who takes up a lot of 'space' – the more you do and say, the greater your influence on group culture. You could try giving yourself a few moments for reflection shortly after a meeting, to replay things that were said and done, and how they might look through someone else's eyes.

Imagining another person's perspective, especially the things they never mention, is never going to give you as accurate information as if they told you about it themselves. Progress is more likely to happen when people start pointing out when they are sidelined or exploited, and bringing perspectives forward that aren't usually heard in the group. Before this happens organically, a lot of people may have left, and others may be exploding with suppressed anger. Whatever position you have in a group, there are a number of things you could try to speed the process. For example, you might have an individual chat with someone about the behaviour you observe and how you feel about it (see the conflict section above for more on this). Alternatively, you might point it out straight away when someone makes assumptions you find even a tiny bit exclusive: ("Some of us have to go to work or drop kids at school – we can't all stay up til late tonight and pay it off with a lie-in in the morning.")

If the group makes it easy for people to give each other feedback and say how they feel, then people are much more likely to voice any concerns early on. The ideas in the above conflict section about creating a supportive culture can help here. For example, you might have a regular slot in your meetings for everyone to say how they feel about the group dynamics. It is important that when someone challenges something that they are respected by the group. Even if you think they are over-reacting, listen carefully and encourage them to explain why they see it in the way they do.

There can be a danger that people who are often in a position of power in a group can want their group to be more diverse simply because they know that this is 'good'. For example, there might be a group opposing cuts to public services, where everyone is able-bodied. If disability benefits is a major issue the group is campaigning on, members might have strong desire to involve some of the people who currently receive those benefits. If this desire leads them to think carefully about the choice of venues and how publicity is made and displayed to ensure maximum accessibility, there are few people who would object. However, if you are a wheelchair user and people are trying to *persuade* you to join their group, or even if you receive an exaggerated welcome at first meeting you turn up to, then you may believe that your visible disability has led them to pick you as a mascot, and feel even less like you can be at home in the group. Each person has the right to decide for themselves whether a group will meet their needs, and the group should respect that.

Sharing out tasks and skills

We identified above that an unequal distribution of tasks was a barrier to people getting involved as equals in decision making. This can be the case when some people do a lot more work than others, and also when the tasks that some people do are accorded more status that others. There are a number of possible responses to this situation. For example:

★ Leaving the distribution of tasks as it is, but trying to change the status that is given to them, for example by thanking the person who took the minutes at a meeting in the same way as the facilitator, or pulling people up when they say things like "Well, I sort of went to the action camp, but I just did the washing up". Be

A Consensus Handbook

aware in this case that ideas about status can be deeply ingrained, and someone might feel more patronised than encouraged!

★ Swapping roles on a regular basis, for example, using a rota system, or setting a rule that someone can only do a particular job once a month.

★ Run skillshares, buddy up on tasks and share key information so that people are supported to take on new roles. When sharing skills informally like this, it would be unusual to plan exactly how to go about it in the way we might if we were running a workshop, but it can help to put some thought into what will help people actually learn. See the short guide on facilitating workshops in the Appendix for some tips.

★ Aim for a balance of the type of tasks each person takes on. For example someone who does lots of facilitation at a gathering could do a little less, and take on cleaning the toilets as well!

A consideration when shifting roles around is whether people have, more or less, enough skills to simply take something on, or whether they need support to learn. In the protest site example we used earlier, it is probably not the end of the world if the food is less good and the log pile grows more slowly for a little while. On the other hand, if everyone gets food poisoning, and someone chops off their foot with an axe, it could be a little more problematic!

However much skillsharing you do the aim is not necessarily to get to a place where everyone spends exactly the same amount of time on each task. It would be a waste if someone was never able to use their talent and passion in a group because they were always making space for other people, or desperately struggling with other tasks

that they were never going to enjoy. We can assume that with enough support to pick up the skills, most people will be able to do an acceptable job at most things. However, you are unlikely to get to the point where everyone is equally able to do any task and if you did you might never do anything else! A simple yardstick to aim for in an established group might be that there is no task that only one person knows how to do, and everyone does some tasks that are considered skilled. Remember that the aim is to take some steps towards evening out your power dynamics, while still achieving whatever it was that your group was set up for, and the distribution of tasks is only one factor in that.

Changing social relationships

Tackling power dynamics can involve changing people's beliefs about themselves and each other. A beautiful presentation of the accounts won't help if people are sat there thinking "What's this got to do with me?" or "Deirdre will decide what we can afford, so why should I get my head round it?". Deep-rooted beliefs may take more time and work to change than this chapter is able to offer tips on, but shifting the ways you relate to each other can help. In meetings, simple things like having a slot for people to talk about feelings, or things that are going on in their lives can help some people. (It can also be very challenging for others, so you might want to limit the time you devote to it, and make it optional!)

Another simple strategy is to spend social time together doing something the group doesn't usually do. Meetings are a very specific way of interacting that work better for some people, and for some sides of people's personalities than for others. If we also socialise together, we can develop greater trust and understanding through knowing each other in different ways. This isn't always straightforward. If you go to the pub and talk about the usual group topics, you may find it doesn't help as much as you hoped. People who don't like sitting in a circle and talking in meetings might not find it a lot easier to join in when the same people are doing the same thing in the pub. The social time only helps if people feel like they can be themselves, and it may make things worse if they don't. For example, if you feel an unease because the group assumption is that everyone is heterosexual and you are not, then if the rest of the group relaxes in the pub and start gossiping about who fancies who it *might* help you bring some things into the open, or you might keep your mouth shut and feel even more estranged. Not to mention that basing your social time on alcohol isn't great for non-drinkers or people who can't afford it. It is best therefore if going to the pub after a meeting is not the default or only option, but one of an array of different contexts in which your relationships are built.

Games let out tensions in different ways, or doing practical activities together, like cooking or walking. If these activities involve an 'expert' to show everyone else what to do then the ideal is for that to be one of the people who is less established in the group. Sometimes it can be easier for people to learn openness and trust through building one on one relationships within a group. Be aware of any-one who is not being included in these activities – an individual's isolation could be increased as informal small group bonding happens between others.

Talking about issues directly

If there is an imbalance in your group, it can help to name it and talk about it directly. For example, maybe some people are putting a lot more time into the group than others. A group where no-one is paid is unlikely to have a way for them to get formal recognition for this. The possibility for guilt and resentment in this situation might be diffused by an explicit conversation about how people feel about it. This might lead into a discussion about how to share tasks more effectively, either immediately, or over the longer term as people's available time fluctuates. On the other hand, it may be that people simply have to accept the imbalance, but are able to do so more easily for having acknowledged it openly.

Whether the power dynamic you see is to do with something specific to your group – like some individuals working harder than others – or whether it is part of a wider social pattern – like people with mental health problems being stigmatised – naming the issue can bring up strong feelings. Mentioning things little and often can help. However, if something has built up to a point where some people feel anxiety about discussing it, then asking for an outside facilitator could be a good idea. If this option isn't available and you ask someone in the group to facilitate, then make sure that everyone trusts them, and that they have time to prepare.

What about when people leave?

You may find that people who don't feel valued in a group don't stick around long enough to let everyone else know how they feel. If you are in the core of a group and notice people leaving, the first thing to remember is that they have every right to do this! You might want more people for your campaign, or it might help you feel good about your group if it manages to be more inclusive, but this isn't their responsibility. However, if you want honest feedback, you could approach the person who has left on an individual basis. Make it clear you're not trying to win them back, but let them know you would welcome them if they did. Check what bits of feedback they are happy for you to pass on to the rest of the group and which they would prefer you didn't. You could ask them how easy it was to speak in meetings and take on tasks. Remember it's not all about you – they may simply have left because it wasn't the right group for them or they realised they didn't have the time or energy. Don't push them beyond what they are comfortable saying – their feedback is a favour to you, and not something they have to do. Prepare yourself not to be defensive if what you hear reflects badly on you or your group, and thank them for helping you out.

Other common issues

External pressures

Consensus works at its best when we can be creative and work together to find new solutions that really work for everyone. However, even if our group dynamics are great, our options can still be limited by external pressures. The political and financial system we live in places a lot of constraints on us that we can't always ignore. If you are a housing co-op looking for somewhere to live, for example, the limited range of buildings you can afford might make it much harder to find something which suits everyone. Even if it was theoretically possible to find a synthesis of different people's ideas by extending and adapting one of the less than ideal buildings, you would still be constrained by planning law, not to mention the limited time left to work on the house once everyone had gone out to work to keep paying off the mortgage and the bills.

If you are in a situation where you are choosing between two bad options, the best thing you can do is be honest about it. Don't tear your group apart battling over which is least terrible. Accept that the problem comes from outside yourselves, and see what you can do to work towards a situation where you have some real control in future. For example, maybe you are a vegetable growing group that has sat on the waiting list for an allotment for several years, and has finally been offered the choice of waiting even longer or taking a small, shady space full of rubble and litter. In the short term you might accept you have to make the best of one of these two options, even if neither are great. However, it helps to recognise that your options would not be so limited in the first place if land was more fairly distributed, and this is the issue which needs to be addressed in the longer term. You might not be able to achieve this on your own, but you could do things in whatever way suited your group to work towards it. This could involve pressurising your local council to provide more allotment spaces, or finding some unused ground that 'belonged' to someone else and planting out your seedlings there.

Chapter 9: *Consensus in wider society* presents some ideas about how society might be differently structured to give us even more real control over the decisions that affect our lives. This wouldn't remove external pressures altogether – our options will always be constrained by what resources are available. When there simply isn't enough to go round any means of making decisions will have its limitations. However, this shouldn't be taken as an excuse to close down the options too quickly! There is usually a fairer way of sharing out what we have, or a creative way of getting more, or the possibility of re-assessing what we really need so that one of the 'bad' options can be made to work – and consensus can help us find our way through all this.

Open groups with changing membership

In a group where there is clear membership, and each person has defined responsibilities, like a co-op or a closed affinity group, then problems can be easier to identify, and there may be more widespread commitment to addressing them. By contrast, in groups that have open membership people often simply disappear if there is an unaddressed conflict, or if they feel there is an inner circle they are excluded from. In other cases someone with limited commitment to a group may push their own views with less concern about what is right for everyone else. The sections above on power dynamics, and creating a supportive culture for a collaborative approach to conflict, provide some ideas about how to create a welcoming group that people don't feel the need to melt away from. This section focuses more on ways the core aims and values of the group can be protected.

What's the problem?

Someone might have their own agenda when they join a group, for example getting involved in a network with a general focus on ecology hoping to get people on board with a more specific campaign – say, against nuclear power. They may have very valid reasons to hold the views that they do, but if these views aren't balanced with a real care for what other people want as well as respect for the core aims of the group then reaching true consensus may become difficult. Or it may simply be that another person has a different understanding of what the group is about. For example, supposing you are an anarchist group that doesn't want to put people off by being too explicit, and simply publicises itself as being into 'empowerment'. This is open to all kinds of interpretation, and may mean that a more diverse range of people come along, but there may not be enough common ground in what they want to do for the group to be useful to anyone. Or perhaps you set up a campaign group that was committed to preventing a new shopping centre from being built in your town. Someone else joins, who is quite positive about the shopping centre, but wants to make sure that it is built in a way that doesn't destroy any of the old buildings on the existing site. You might be able to work with this person on specific issues, but if they joined your group and had a significant influence on the direction it took, you might find that soon there was no group left that was actually opposed to the shopping centre. Therefore, as well as supporting new people to become included, you may want to find ways to protect the group's core aims and activities so that it is not prevented from doing and being what it was set up for.

Protecting the group

As always, there is a question of striking the right balance between protecting the group and its aims, yet being open to new ideas and people. There is limited benefit to a group that is so dominated by what the founding members wanted that it can't adapt to changes in circumstances, or new people can never have an influence on what it does. However, there are a few simple strategies that can make sure everyone has a grasp of what the original vision was, and changes come about through conscious decisions rather than drifting along or misunderstandings.

Learning from closed groups

More formal groups often have systems in place to keep the group true to its original intentions. It is common for a co-op to have a structured joining process for people who are new to work out if the group is right for them and vice versa. During this period, there may be limitations on the influence the newcomer can have on the group and its direction. For example, probationary members might only be able to contribute to short term decisions which will definitely affect them, but not to a longer term strategy. Or they might be allowed to give their opinion, but not to block a decision from going ahead until their probationary period was over. A more open group, the membership of which is made up of people who happened to turn up at any particular meeting, would find it hard to put structures like this in place. It would be possible to have rules saying something like people had to attend at least two meetings before they could have certain rights in the group – like using the block or joining the email list. However, this might be more off-putting than it was useful! Other possibilities are setting rules which limit the use of the block for everybody – saying that it can only be used to protect the core aims of the group, and not for individual reasons, for example.

Clear communication with newcomers

Any group can use some simple ways of protecting itself and its activities. The suggestions below are less about introducing rules and procedures, and more about how you communicate about the group and what it stands for.

Be clear what the core goals and shared principles of the group are. Explain these in any publicity and tell new people when they come, along with anything else they need to know about how the group works. Don't overdo it – lots of people don't like being bombarded with information when they first arrive somewhere. On the other hand it is not particularly empowering to be left trying to work out what is going on, or to only find out what the group's views are when you say something different and an awkward silence falls. Pace the information you give, and balance it with an interest in the new people and who they are. If someone suggests something which goes against the group's beliefs and aims, it is usually better to say so openly than go silent and leave them guessing what they've done wrong.

It is particularly important to **make sure everyone understands how you make decisions.** Don't just explain the process (or worse, just the hand-signals!) that you use when making a consensus decision – be clear about the principles behind it. You might need to give this explanation at the beginning of the meeting and repeat it at the decision making stage. Be especially careful that everyone understands how your group uses blocks, stand asides etc. This is worth doing even if someone has used consensus before. It is less likely to seem patronising if you frame it in terms of different groups having different ways of making consensus decisions, and show a genuine interest in any variations that they have met.

Record the decisions you make, and refer back to them whenever a related item comes up so that you aren't unnecessarily revisiting past decisions. For example, imagine a group has already had a long discussion about how to present their campaign in a way that made clear links with other issues. You might not be exactly the same set of people next time you come to make a leaflet or prepare a media interview, and you may well make different decisions, but it can be helpful to all look at what was decided last time and why, so you make use of the work and thought that has already gone into it. Think carefully about which decisions are open to review when someone new comes along. For example, an anti-militarist group that did direct action at army bases and weapons manufacturers might have some standard security procedures to make sure they got to do their actions before anyone came to stop them. They might simply explain these to new people and expect them to either agree or leave, or they might decide it was worth starting from scratch when someone new joined so that everyone was fully on board with what was agreed.

What if you're the only person who wants the group to change?

A lot of the advice in this book is written for the benefit of a whole group. But, what if you are in a group where other people don't know about, or aren't interested in consensus? Another common situation is for a group to say that they use consensus, but without wanting to make any real changes in order to properly involve everyone in decision making. If you are just one person, or a small minority that has a different view, then your options for making the changes you would like to see are more limited.

Questions to ask yourself

Is consensus right for the group, or is it just something that you would like to see happen? If the group has made a conscious decision to use a different method of decision making, you could explain why you didn't agree, but you probably couldn't change what they did. In a group where people hadn't really thought about how to make decisions, it might be easier to persuade them, but this might be an abuse of your power, or at least a waste of your time. Refer back to the conditions for consensus, and think about whether you can imagine them ever being met. For example, maybe the group has been set up with a particular purpose – like setting up a community orchard or opposing a new road, and for most people this objective will always be much more important than the internal group dynamics. Therefore, even if people agree to use consensus, or say they already do, it may never get a high enough priority for them to change how they hold their meetings. Alternatively, perhaps you have a formal role in the group which gives you the 'right' to introduce something new – like being the president of the Student Union, a teacher overseeing a school council or a volunteer who runs a youth group. In this case the question is whether the people you are introducing it to have the power to make meaningful decisions themselves – if you or someone else has the final word then it is best to be honest about this and only use consensus when everyone really does get involved as an equal, and the group does have the power to make decisions.

What are you going to do about it?

Thinking about these questions on your own might be enough for you to decide the group will never work by consensus. If consensus is a big priority for you, you might decide you want leave, or you might stick around because the other things the group does are important to you. If you stick around, you could still make some suggestions about more democratic ways of working. For example, a group could continue to use voting, but pay greater attention to including everyone in the discussion. Alternatively, it might be that there are a number of people who seem interested in using consensus, as well as others who are more sceptical, or just not interested. In this case, you might decide to look at where the group is at currently, and make a few suggestions about how to improve the dynamics. Alternatively, you might present your entire vision for how group decision making could work and why. This might inspire some people and be totally dismissed by others – use your judgement as to what would work best in your own group.

Sharing your thoughts

If the issue seems to be that people follow the rhetoric of consensus but are actually too attached to their own power to really apply it, then look back at the sections on power, privilege and conflict for thoughts on how to deal with the issue. On the other hand, if the issue is that people lack knowledge and experience of consensus, you can find ways to share yours. Make sure that anything you say is in the spirit of offering suggestions and observations, but not trying to convince them that you are right. If they don't share your values you can't force them to, you can just explain what you think. Try to explain the principles of consensus in a way that enables people to think about what they believe without being too loaded. If you say for example, "Voting allows minorities to be steamrollered into silence – anyone who truly respects other people uses consensus" then people who have used voting all their life may not feel that this is a fair representation of their own behaviour. It might be more effective to say something more neutral like, "When a group votes anyone in a minority position is over-ruled, whereas consensus looks for options everyone can live with."

Observations on how meetings are happening may help people see different ways of doing things. To begin with it can help to express this in a way that doesn't comment directly on individuals, e.g. "I notice that people are speaking different amounts" is easier to swallow than "Juan dominates the group". (This doesn't mean you should brush it under the carpet if Juan continues to do all the talking – look at the conflict section above for ideas about how to bring it up.) Link your observations to alternative suggestions, e.g. "Maureen said she thought the community centre was the best venue and a few people nodded and now we seem to be assuming it has been agreed. I think it might be helpful to check whether everyone really is happy with this venue. That way we know we actually did have consensus, and we can write it down knowing that it was a clear decision."

Limit the number of suggestions and observations that you make in order not to create an unhealthy dynamic. If some individuals in the group are interested you might want to talk to them more about your ideas, but avoid creating a faction of people who back each other up on things they've already talked about outside the meeting. For example, if you have a private discussion with someone about the group dynamics, and you encourage them to bring it to a meeting, be honest with yourself about whether your intention is to empower them or to get someone else to voice your ideas. If they had said something you didn't agree with would you be equally encouraging?

A better strategy might be to get someone in from the outside. For example, you might think there are lots of things the group could do to improve their facilitation skills, but worry that they might not listen to these ideas coming from you. Getting someone from another group to run a workshop might help people to be open to new ideas which they can think about for themselves.

A conclusion

Many groups choose consensus because they want to work together as equals, using the full creative power of everyone involved. Some groups call their decision making process 'consensus' simply because they don't vote. However, in order to achieve the meaningful consent of everyone in a group, all those people need to be interacting as equals, and taking shared responsibility for how the decision gets made as well as what the outcome is, even when their interests appear to be in conflict. It is easy to feel disillusioned, or even betrayed, if you feel that your group is not even attempting to do this work. Most of us experience frustration when progress is slow or uneven. However, it is also possible to look at the situation the other way round: it is when we succeed in a difficult situation, that consensus can have a transformative power.

When there is real commitment to doing consensus we experience respect and understanding, not just from the people who are close to us and 'on our side', but from a wider group that may not agree with us, or even like us. Trust and openness were listed in the first chapter as conditions for consensus. However, the reverse can also be true. By experiencing good consensus processes we can learn to be trusting and open. We can learn – whatever our life experience of trying to prove ourselves, of trying to win people over, of suppressing our own needs in order to fit in – that there are many other possibilities out there. It is possible to honestly express what we want, and have it taken on board by people who want something different. It is possible to experience powerful anger, and still listen to the perspectives of the person who triggered that anger. It is possible to let go of the control we have had over a group, and share that control *with* the group instead. Experiencing these things opens the door to another way of living and to different kinds of community. There is no time like the present to start learning how.

Chapter 9:
Consensus in wider society

**The rest of this book comes from our own experiences of facilit-
ating consensus in groups of between two people and several
thousand. Equality, freedom, shared responsibility, respect: by
using consensus in our groups we learn to make these abstract
principles a bit more real in our day to day decision making.** We
can carve out a little space in which we experience both the challenges and the fulfilment of empowerment and co-operation.
However, the scope of our decision making is limited: these groups
are relatively small and self-selected, making decisions on just a
small range of specific questions. In other areas of our life we simply
have to fit ourselves as best we can around the rules of the powers
that be. We have little or no control in important decisions like
whether our tax money should fund wars, whether the local Accident
and Emergency hospital department should stay open or how public
education should work.

This chapter looks at how the principles of consensus might be applied in the whole of society, so we can all have true involvement in
these fundamental decisions. If, in your head, you are now trying to
marry up the process you use to make decisions in your small group
with the institutions that run the world today, the mismatch will be
pretty mind-boggling. Clearly we cannot replace the United Nations
by getting everyone in the world to sit in a huge circle and do a nine
billion person go-round on every issue that comes up. Nor would it
greatly help if we were to change national parliaments so they used
consensus with each other to make laws – their interests would still

A Consensus Handbook

be very remote from the people they were supposed to represent. This chapter, therefore, is less about how to run our individual meetings and more about how society could be fundamentally restructured to make direct democracy possible.

Below, we present some ideas to show how society could be organised around the principles of consensus. This is no manifesto: even for ourselves there are no definitive answers, and we're certainly not setting out to tell you what the world *should* look like. However, without thinking about how things *could* be done, abstract principles like equality and freedom remain exactly that – attractive words with no real meaning. Therefore, we're using this space to try out some more concrete ideas for how decision making could work in wider society. These serve as a springboard for thinking about some of the challenges we might face in putting our principles into practice and some possible ways these challenges could be tackled. We encourage you to think critically about these things too. Think and talk and listen and argue with us and read and write and agitate for change and try things out on whatever scale you can.

Case study: Participatory budgeting

Even within the current system, there is some recognition that the more control people have over the decisions that affect them, the better the decisions are made, and the more able people are to accept the outcomes. For example, participatory budgeting was first developed in Porto Alegre, a Brazilian city of 1.3 million inhabitants. This is a year long process in which the residents of the city make decisions about how to allocate city council spending. First people get together in neighbourhoods to decide what local needs are and to elect delegates to district forums. These forums then create a list of priorities for expenditure and elect two members for a city-wide Municipal Budget Council, which works out how to distribute the available funds between districts. Systems like this have their limitations – people are 'given' control over a relatively small proportion of decisions that affect them, and it is the city wide council, not the neighbourhood meetings that have the final say. Even given these limitations, participatory budgeting goes a lot further than the systems which usually get called democratic, and reportedly has resulted in much more equitable public spending.

Is it possible?

Consensus requires us to behave in very different ways from the competitive norms of capitalist society. Even in small, close-knit groups people can find it hard to stop trying to win. It is easy to assume that the behaviour that we see around you every day represents human nature – that people act like they do because that is what people will always be like. However, it is hard to judge whether that is true or not if you live in a culture that actively *encourages* competition. Getting into college, finding work and somewhere to live, persuading someone they want to share their bed or their life with you... in all these significant areas of life, we are encouraged to believe that our success depends on someone else's failure. It seems fair to assume that in a political system which encourages co-operation and responsibility, people might behave quite differently.

This is not making any arguments at all about whether human nature is intrinsically 'good' or 'bad'. Quite the opposite, it is recognising that most of us are capable of extremes of both selfishness and emotional generosity. We feel it is significant that different human societies uphold different values – for example the expectations around how much we share 'personal' wealth with people around us will vary greatly depending on the culture we live in. If we lived in a society that encouraged and valued shared responsibility, empathy and co-operation it seems likely we would be more responsible, more empathetic and more co-operative, even if we were still *capable* of competitive behaviour. Consensus, with its emphasis on sharing power and finding win-win solutions, has the potential to bring out this capacity for responsibility, empathy and co-operation. Certainly, we shouldn't limit our imagination to the political and economic systems operating in the world today: it's not a very long time since the dominant view in British culture was that women and working class people weren't intelligent enough to be educated or that colonial rule was inevitable and necessary.

It's not just our own culture and behaviour that help limit the possibilities for change – the powers that shape the world we live in also wield a massive influence. However, events like the so-called Arab Spring (since 2010) demonstrate how much frustration is simmering under the surface. The system we know is not nearly as stable as they would have us believe. Few predicted the widespread impact of the many serious economic crises in the last 100 years: the 1929 Wall St. crash, the 1973 oil crisis, the bank collapse of Iceland in 2008 or the Eurozone crisis starting in 2010 to name just a few. Given the increasing scarcity of the resources on which the global economy is built (like oil, for instance) it seems likely more upheaval is to come. Instability opens the door to the possibility of major change – whether for better or worse remains to be seen, but this makes it all the more important that we start thinking now about what 'better' might look like and what we could do to get there.

So how might it work?

When consensus was first introduced in Chapter 1 we used the analogy of a group of friends going out for a meal – there was no point in a majority vote to eat pizza if that excluded the coeliac and the vegan. Supposing the question was slightly more important – how should a town prioritise its resources – should more go on education, health care, or transport, for example? As things stand, the vast majority of the population has very little influence on these issues. Clearly such questions are more complicated to resolve than where to go out to eat – the decisions involve many more factors, many more people, much greater diversity of opinion and the consequences are wider-reaching and more significant. We will very probably find it almost impossible to reach the perfect synthesised outcome, where everyone is truly happy with the final decision. On the other hand, because these are wide-reaching decisions with important consequences, and because there aren't any perfect solutions, there is all the more reason for everyone to have the option of involvement. It is much easier to accept a decision if you have been part of making it, feel your opinion has been heard, and understand how that decision came about.

This still leaves practical questions, however – we have already said that we couldn't get everyone in the world, or even one country, into one room to thrash out every issue together. The same is true even of a town. So how can that involvement in day to day decision making be achieved? Each community must come to its own conclusions about how to make decisions together, but we have laid out some basic organisational principles that we think would be necessary for any kind of direct democracy to work at a societal level. We then follow with a more detailed model of one possible way of structuring decision making.

Organisational principles

Decentralisation: Decisions should be made by those that are affected by them. Only those with a legitimate interest in a decision should have an input. The more local and decentralised our decision making is, the more possible it is to get involved in the decisions that affect our lives.

Diversity is our strength: We all have different needs and desires. To accommodate these we need to create a fluid society full of diversity, allowing each to find their niche – creating a richly patterned quilt rather than forcing people into the same bland uniform. The more varied the society we create, the more stable it will be.

Case study: Community self organisation

In Argentina in 2001, a major economic crisis and a popular uprising unseated four governments in succession. International media covered food rioting and looting that broke out as a result. However, alongside this, were many examples of self-governance and co-operation under extreme pressure. Workplaces that had been abandoned by their owners were taken over by workers and turned into co-operatives – from schools to a newspaper to the massive ceramics factory Zanon. Barter clubs cropped up as the currency collapsed. In the absence of government or state services, people met in weekly neighbourhood assemblies to discuss pressing issues, and organise support for people in the community, for example, setting up soup kitchens or preventing the eviction of squatting workers' co-ops. These assemblies then split into 'committees' that took on jobs like organising health care. And every Sunday, spokespeople from each assembly met in an inter-neighbourhood plenary that reported back on what was going on in local areas, and developed strategies for city-wide mobilisations against the government.

Respect and co-operation between groups: Some decisions have a far-reaching impact. For example, when we use scarce resources, or cause pollution, what we do affects people who live far away. Sometimes groups can achieve a lot more collaborating across a wide geographical area – for example several hospitals sharing a very specialised piece of equipment. Decentralisation doesn't have to mean complete atomisation if groups collaborate to ensure equality and fairness on a wider scale.

Clear and understandable structures: While we need the fabric of our society to be complex, we want the structures for organising and making decisions to be simple and understandable. It needs to be easy for people to engage in decision-making.

Accountability: If you know you are accountable to people around you it means you have to take responsibility for your actions. This makes it more difficult to accumulate power or play ego games and avoids corruption – common pitfalls of organising on any scale. Accountability is easier to achieve in a decentralised society, with decisions being made at the local level by the groups of people affected by them. Where we need co-operation on a larger scale, it becomes even more important that decision making processes are easily understood, transparent and open. That way there can be greater accountability even within much bigger groups.

Case study: Workers' collectives

The remarkable events of the Spanish Revolution in 1936 were the culmination of decades of popular education and agitation. During the civil war, large parts of the country were organised in decentralised and collective ways. A famous example is the Barcelona General Tramway Co. which was deserted by its managers. The 7000 workers took over the running of the trams, with different collectives running the trams for different parts of the city. Citywide services were maintained by federalist co-ordination.

The increased efficiency of the collectives led to an operating surplus, despite running more trams, cutting fares, increasing wages and getting new equipment! The general spirit was one of optimism and freedom.

A basic model

So what would this society look like? How could these these principles be put into practice? How could services be organised, limited resources shared out, conflicts resolved? How could health care, public transport, the post work?

A common model for structuring society is using neighbourhoods and workers' collectives as two basic units for decision-making. Within the neighbourhoods people co-operate to provide themselves with services such as food distribution and waste disposal. Workers' collectives take on projects such as running a bus service, factories, shops, hospitals.

These neighbourhoods would involve a fairly small group of people –

Case study: Federalist co-ordination

It can be hard to imagine how services such as train travel or bus services through several communities can be organised without a central authority, particularly if each community is independent and organised by its residents rather than a central government.

On the other hand it can be relatively easy to work out how some services between communities can work: the postal service for example could work much as it currently does between countries. It's not important how each community decides to organise delivery of letters and parcels, or how much a stamp costs (or whether stamps are even used) – the main thing is that there are agreements in place for accepting and passing on post for other areas.

Other services such as trains can work in the same way, but obviously need more negotiation: there are timetabling, safety issues and inter-regional standards of track and rolling stock to be agreed. But once again, we already have international agreements in place that show how infrastructure services between socially and economically independent entities are possible.

A Consensus Handbook

perhaps all the people who lived on one floor of a very big tower block, a cluster of houses in a rural area, or a group of travellers who went round together. For the sake of this example, we have imagined that the neighbourhoods are streets in a smallish town: *Utopaville*.

In Utopaville, decisions in all these groups, (the neighbourhoods and workers' collectives) are made by direct democracy, each member being directly involved in making the decisions affecting their lives. Some of these groups might vote, others operate by consensus but all are characterised by respect for everyone and the desire to find solutions that are agreeable to all. It may sound as if we'd have to spend all our time in committees and meetings, but organising on a local level is made much easier through daily personal contact, meaning that most things could be worked out through informal and spontaneous discussion and co-operation.

Even the street or workplace may not be the smallest working unit. Just as workplaces can have working groups for publicity or purchasing, a street may have a working group for looking after a common resource, like laundry facilities, or street lamp maintenance. The people within that working group may have an agreed budget to carry out repairs and buy new washing machines, or they may have to take it to the street meeting. Either way, something as low level as maintaining the laundry facilities should be looked after by people living in small units, such as the street, rather than require everyone in a town or city to get involved (although streets may decide to co-operate and share facilities or repairs, for example).

Something like disposal of waste (whether that's glass recycling or human faeces) will probably need to be agreed between more people. One street could agree to leave raw sewage outside their houses, but this might quickly become a health hazard for other people living near them. Because everyone in the town is potentially affected, there's a strong argument for agreement on minimum standards. Naturally in this case everyone will need to have a say in what is decided. This is where some kind of decision making structure such as a spokescouncil will be useful (see Chapter 3: *Facilitating consensus in large groups*).

In our model town Utopaville there are 100 roads (or sections of roads, streets, cul-de-sacs etc), each with approximately 10 dwellings. Each house and flat has an average of 4 people in it. That makes 1000 dwellings and 4000 people. Imagine the fun our 4000 residents would have if they were all in a big hall talking about how to deal with human poo! Even if only half the people had any interest in the issue at all, there'd still be 2000 people crammed into the room wanting to talk about smell and hygiene and water use and soil fertility and composting.

But if each street first considered the issue, then sent one or two spokespeople to represent their views to a spokescouncil we'd have just 100 people trying to speak at our meeting. That's still a lot, but it's 40 times better than 4000! There may also be other ways we can break down the meeting further: the geography of the town might naturally break down into areas. Let's imagine there are four such areas in our Utopaville (south of the river, on the hill, in the valley and the north bank) – each area can come to agreement between the 25 spokes and their 25 streets about how to deal with the sewage. Every so often one or two people from a spokescouncil can check in with the other three spokescouncils that the ideas they're coming up with are compatible with and acceptable to the other three areas. This could be a second tier spokescouncil (see page 73), which regularly meets and is made up with two members of each of the first tier spokescouncils (i.e. 8 people). There might even be a need for the people of Utopaville to check that their solutions to the poo problem are acceptable to people in other towns and villages in the area (e.g. those sharing an aquifer or water source). This could involve a third tier spokescouncil, where one or two residents of Utopaville met up with people from other towns and villages. In this case, the views of the people in each street in each town would be fed up through the different tiers to the regional spokescouncil.

There are some questions in life which have even wider reaching impacts than the disposal of excrement. For example, greenhouse gas emissions or the use of very scarce resources. Co-operation may be needed over huge geographical areas – even globally. Further tiers of spokescouncils could be used to bring together the views of people living in many different regions.

Clearly the most important part of the spokescouncil system is that the spokes are only speaking, negotiating or agreeing with the full knowledge and consent of everyone involved. A group might require that their spoke checks back any decision made, or they might

Case study: Community organisation

If you visit Christiania in the heart of Copenhagen, and get past the touristy parts near the main gate, you'll see people organising their housing and their workplaces. You might see maintenance teams looking after the infrastructure that make living and working in Christiania possible: paths being repaired, utility pipes and cables being renewed.

The starting point for all social organisation in Christiania is simply that every individual has a responsibility for their own life and home.

The next level of organising is the **Area Meeting.** The Freetown is made up of 14 areas which together work out the practicalities of maintaining their area, decide on admitting new residents and deal with any problems between residents.

If a problem can't be solved, it is referred to the **Community Meeting**, which meets as often as is needed. The Community Meeting deals with all questions which affect the whole of the Freetown, and any Christianite may participate.

empower them to make decisions on their behalf. Either way, there needs to be mechanisms in place to make sure that important decisions get made and that delegates remain directly answerable to their group and don't become unofficial leaders. Devices like rotating the spoke at frequent intervals can help avoid power building up. For example, the Camps for Climate Action in Britain from 2006 – 2010 used a system whereby two spokes were sent from local groups to spokescouncil meetings each day – one person who had attended the day before to ensure continuity, and one person who was new to it. The following day the person who had been new would go along as the experienced old hand to help out the next new person. In a longer term system spokes might not have to change every meeting, but the same basic idea of overlapping rotation of delegates could be followed.

This makes it all sound like a lot of work, a lot of to-ing and fro-ing between local level and the spokescouncils, but it's worth bearing in mind that there's likely to be a lot of talking and thinking when we first start to deal with the questions, like how to empty our toilets, but once a system is in place we'll only need to meet at town level when things aren't working properly (e.g. the compost heap is too big), or every so often to double check that everything is working properly. Similarly, to make sure the whole structure doesn't get unwieldy and over-centralised, spokescouncils representing a wider area could make very broad brush policy decisions, leaving the details of implementation to more localised areas. For example, if a spokescouncil agreed an acceptable average level of greenhouse gas emissions per person, decisions could be made in towns about how much of that allocation got taken up by hospitals or public transport, and streets could work out how to divide up the allocation that was left to them – whether to do things like cooking and laundry together for the sake of efficiency, whether people with certain disabilities should get priority, etc. Or, returning to the poo example, on a day to day basis, the street may decide that each house is usually responsible for delivering the contents of their compost toilets to their street composting facility. Then each street sets up working groups for things like keeping an eye on the compost heap, turning it when necessary, and carting it out to the area orchards when the poo is safely composted down. Exactly who is on the composting rota, and how they are held accountable to their street(s) is a decision to be made by the streets, not the composting spokescouncil.

A Consensus Handbook

Challenges, questions and tensions

We started this chapter with a set of basic principles: **freedom, equality, shared responsibility, co-operation** and **respect**. The model that we offer above attempts to show how these might be put into practice – by using a system of decentralised groups, co-ordinating via spokescouncils where necessary, people are able to share control over the decisions that affect their lives. However, if we dig a little deeper, we can see a number of challenges we might face trying to put these principles into practice. We don't believe that these challenges invalidate the model we have offered – however a society makes decisions, there will always be difficult questions to face. Honest discussion about these tensions puts us all in a better place to come up with new ideas, or ways of making things work.

Can our society be both equal and free?

Many people, if asked whether they thought equality and freedom were good things, wouldn't have too much difficulty in saying *yes*. However, in practice, having both at the same time is not always so straightforward. People use the word freedom to demand the right to do all kinds of things, like carry a gun or drive fast down residential streets. Yet it is pretty clear that a gun or a car hold the potential to entirely take away someone else's freedom – to take their life in fact. These things may represent freedom for the individual wanting to do them. But, if everyone has the automatic right to do whatever they want without checking in with anyone else it doesn't create a free *society*: one person's freedom may come at the expense of others.

The idea is that having a society based on consensus reconciles this tension. As well as being a way of organising in groups (setting up a communal compost toilet system, in our example), consensus can be a tool for resolving conflict. We can assume that in our society, everyone is free to do what they want until that interferes with other people, at which point they use consensus to negotiate a solution. This negotiation happens directly with the other people affected instead of having law-makers and police intervening. Because we share responsibility for finding a synthesised solution that everyone is truly happy with, or at least a compromise everyone can voluntarily accept, we remain free, but free amongst equals. For example, one person can enjoy the freedom to play music loud in the dead of night, and respect their neighbour's equal right to peaceful sleep, if they soundproof their walls well. Even on a global scale negotiations could be set up – for example, between people who wanted to use uranium in the treatment of cancer, and the people who lived near the potential mines and were concerned by the evidence that excavation would *cause* them cancer.

However, sometimes the other people affected aren't around to let us know that there is a problem and negotiate with us. It is hard to imagine the person who wants to use a gun to defend their house inviting potential burglars over for a reasonable chat about whether they think the use of firearms is justifiable or not. Or suppose a group comes to a 'consensus' decision to dig up the local peat bog in order to fertilise their vegetable patch. The impacts of climate change are so widely recognised that we can imagine other people wanting to get involved in this decision. We can also imagine the people down the road who wanted to burn the peat to heat their homes having a view on the matter. However, the decision also impacts on the wildlife that is currently supported by the peat bog, but a butterfly or a marsh harrier is not able to invite the group to a meeting to reach an agreement.

A Consensus Handbook

Therefore, a culture that values freedom and equality doesn't just require us to have meetings with our neighbours about the emptying of compost toilets or the communal laundry. The more things we do that have far reaching impacts, the greater the need to set up negotiations between different groups and individuals. This requires proactive behaviour – to approach others when what you want to do might affect them, or when what they are doing impacts on you.

Living things that are not human adults also need protection. Some people have suggested appointing advocates for things like ecosystems or future generations who can't make it to the meeting in person. The challenge then is how to reach agreement on what living things should be represented, and how seriously to take their needs. For example, it is generally accepted that what we eat is a matter for individual choice, and we shouldn't interfere with what someone else does. However, the pig sitting on our neighbour's plate didn't get the chance to offer its informed consent before being made into bacon, and there are certainly people who would like to withhold that consent on its behalf. People who are opposed to abortion would probably make the same argument about a foetus. These examples are deliberately controversial – the pig advocates may not be the same as those supporting the foetus. Other people will not be particularly bothered by either, but will want to defend trees, or young children, or ancient buildings. The desire to make everyone do the thing you think is right is tempered by the desire not to be made to do things that other people think are right.

Of course, this kind of moral conflict is not unique to a consensus society. In Britain today there are laws restricting some of the things people might want to do, but there are many areas where, if we want someone to stop doing something, our only option is to ask them. People with strong views on anything today are faced with the same dilemmas as they would have in a more utopian society – torn between conflicting pressures of social conditioning ("Don't cause trouble, it'll be embarrassing,") personal morality (on the one hand: "Other people have the right to their own choices," on the other: "What they're doing is wrong,") and concerns about what kinds of interference will actually be effective. In a culture where direct negotiation is a normal response to disagreement, the conversations might be a little more productive, but still we all have to live with the fact that even in our utopia other people will keep doing some things we'd rather they didn't and will possibly want to stop us doing some of things we think are perfectly reasonable. The only political system that would give absolute expression of our own belief system would be ourselves as absolute dictator. The alternative we propose is respectful dialogue even when we have profoundly opposing viewpoints. For each individual this is likely to result in some frustration and imperfect compromises. However, if that respectful dialogue can be achieved, then for a society as a whole it may be the best response to a muddy reality.

What happens when we can't agree?

The examples above suggest that in cases of ethical conflict there will be times when we can't find a synthesised solution everyone is happy with, or even a compromise that everyone can accept. This is likely to be the case also when we have more practical disagreements and incompatibilities, like what hygiene standards should be applied in the communal kitchen or how to use a limited water supply.

Splitting groups as a solution

We named diversity as one of the basic organising principles of a democratic society. Rather than trying to come to the same agreement about how to live with lots of people, we can divide up into different streets, villages or towns according to significant things we have in common. This is particularly appropriate if the incompatibilities between us were limited to a particular thing that we share. For example, the people who disagreed about hygiene in the kitchen could be perfectly friendly neighbours provided they didn't cook in the same space. There could be two workers' collectives that did the same job, but with very different working styles – one very flexible with a lot of last minute rushes, the other with regular hours and careful scheduling. One town might respond to global limitations on greenhouse gas emissions by developing low impact technology, while another group of people choose a lifestyle based on foraging for food and fuel. The option to choose like-minded communities supports social stability – there is much less occasion for conflict if society as a whole creates welcoming spaces for people with a wide range of different views and needs.

However, if the issue is not so much an incompatibility in how you do things as some people feeling that something shouldn't happen at all, division of a group can have limited benefit as a solution. To return to the examples above, if you think that pigs should not be eaten by humans it probably doesn't make a lot of difference to you where they are eaten, and moving somewhere where you don't have to see it happen may not help. Someone who believes that the human foetus has rights probably believes it about all of them, and not just the ones that are conceived by women living on their street. Or supposing that a large majority of people in a village felt that all land should be owned and controlled collectively. A small group of people who have been farming particular bits of land in their own way for years are very resistant to the idea. When successive meetings have failed to bring any resolution, it is suggested they leave the village to allow the decision to go ahead. This might not greatly placate them – the attachment is to 'their' land rather than a particular model of land ownership, and no other place could provide that.

Additionally, splitting a group could cause major trauma. We don't necessarily want to choose where we live or work based on questions like people's approach to meetings or washing up. Communities will not always be formed around things we have in common – some are likely to grow up in the more organic ways that have been common across human history – who falls in love with whom, where there is water and fertile land, or places to work. Splitting groups because people disagree could mean leaving those people they fell in love with, leaving their friends, leaving the place with the water and land or the factory they set up and with no guarantee of somewhere else to go.

Different ways of making decisions

Groups that struggle to reach consensus might choose to use a different means of making decisions. For example, imagine trying to reach agreement in a large town – some people might find it hard to swallow the idea that one person could block a decision that 999,999 people had accepted. Alternatives could range from a simple majority vote, (if more than 50% agree it's OK), to a vote requiring a larger majority, to 'consensus-minus-one' where a single blocker can be ignored, but the consent of everyone else needs to be secured. Some groups might use these methods all the time, for others it could be a fallback, for example if three successive meetings have failed to reach consensus, they might switch to a super-majority vote.

Using methods other than consensus might enable the group as a whole to reach decisions and therefore keep functioning as a community. On the other hand, for individuals concerned, the outcomes may be the same as if the group split as a response to unresolved conflict. A dissenting minority that felt so strongly they would have blocked a consensus decision may find that leaving is their best option when they are over-ruled in a vote. Or, if they stay, their commitment to the community and its decision making processes may be reduced. In looking at what decision-making method to use, a community will need to balance the need to reach an agreement more quickly (or at all!) so they can move forward, and the need to maintain the trust and commitment of everyone concerned. The discussions below on enforcing decisions and efficiency feed into the question of how to find this balance.

A Consensus Handbook

Enforcing decisions

If we make a decision with a group of people we need to trust that it will be implemented. Suppose we get together with people from a few villages to work out a fair way of sharing the water that comes into the valley – how much should go to schools and health centres, and how much to private homes, for example. What happens if one group starts syphoning off more than their agreed share to fill a swimming pool? Or maybe a childcare collective makes an agreement that no-one should hit the children, but some adults start lashing out when they get stressed. The theory of consensus is that when people are involved in making a decision, they are more likely to implement it – they had the opportunity to withdraw their consent when the decision was made and if they didn't take it at that time, then they will stick to what was agreed. Compared to the political system most of us live in today, this is probably a fair assumption. The people our society names as criminals are often alienated, disenfranchised and exploited. Those lawbreakers less likely to be identified as criminals (e.g.: large-scale tax evaders) enjoy the near-immunity from punishment that comes with extreme power and wealth. In a society where everyone is empowered as equals, then people are more likely to be able to see each other's common humanity, and implement decisions with honesty.

However, it is one thing to say that reasons for law breaking in our society today include social inequality and a lack of widespread involvement in decision making. This does not mean we can assume that if those issues could be removed, there would never be any other reasons why people went back on an agreement that had been made. Anyone who has any experience of group organising is likely to be familiar with 'agreed to do it but didn't get around to it' scenario. Or the situation where everyone agrees to something one person wants for the sake of a quiet life, but without any real intention of following through with it. When decisions affect many more people, it becomes harder to truly involve everyone, and the risk that people will not all be brought into the decisions becomes higher. A tiered spokescouncil allows input from a lot of people, but they may still feel far removed from the group who finally sit together in a room and thrash out an agreement. Imagine a decision was made

through such a spokescouncil that coal should be left in the ground. If people in one village knew where a coal seam lay close to the surface, it seems possible that in a cold winter at least some people would go out at night with their spade and 'liberate' some of the coal.

So how do we deal with this? If we simply shrug our shoulders and walk away when we see agreements not being kept to, we break the entire system of trust on which our decision making and our society is based. Who would sit in a meeting trying to reach agreement, if they thought that others were going to do what they wanted regardless? Without commitment to keeping to agreements there is no point in making decisions together, and a system of organised co-operation between equals becomes a system of competitive individualism.

The alternative used by most political systems today is to try to prevent infringements of their rules with the threat of punishment – we can be fined or imprisoned (or in some places executed), and if we resist we can be restrained and intimidated with an array of weapons from truncheons, dogs and tear gas to guns, depending on who we are and what we (try to) do. This system is problematic on a number of levels – firstly, that using force to punish people doesn't really follow the values of freedom and equality which we said were the basis of our consensus society. On a more practical level, when we formally empower one group of people to use violence against another, we lay the door open to corruption and oppression. And even if we believe these risks and ethical compromises are acceptable, there is still the question of whether punishment works as well as 'they' claim. Fear of getting caught might stop people from shop-lifting but is it really the fine they are worried about or the social embarrassment? And is it really the threat of punishment that prevents people from doing more serious things like rape? The figures often quoted in England and Wales for example, are that only one in ten rapes are reported, and of those only 6% lead to a conviction, suggesting that the risk of punishment is relatively small. In a consensus system we rely on most people willingly sticking to agreements. Using punishment as a back up might help restrain a few individuals, but could actively undermine the trust and goodwill that led others to comply.

Sharing responsibility for creating an accountable culture might be more effective. For example, meetings could regularly check that everyone was doing what they said they would do, and everyone could feel empowered to point out to someone that they weren't sticking to agreements. Knowing that what we do is noticed by our peers may encourage much more responsibility for our actions than punishment by authority, which seems to breed an attitude of "It's OK so long as I don't get caught." Of course, fear of embarrassment can be a problematic way of controlling people's behaviour, the same as more formal punishments are. Offering to re-open a decision when observing someone who isn't keeping to it is more respectful, even if not always very realistic. A complementary approach is to do more to build up the trust and goodwill that means people are more likely to voluntarily abide by decisions. After all, if people regularly break agreements, it is likely to be a sign that the conditions for consensus aren't in place. A lot can be achieved by improving facilitation, thinking critically about who needs to be involved in each decision, tackling unhealthy power dynamics and addressing conflict constructively so as to increase true involvement in decision making.

However, the likelihood is that all groups will need to have some options available when a decision is not stuck to, or someone is doing something that others find totally unacceptable, and refuses to stop. This need might be greater in a group that has, for example, minimised feed in process to a spokescouncil in order to speed up meeting times, or uses other ways of making decisions (like a majority vote). Nevertheless, however high a priority a group gives to inclusion, we can assume that sometimes agreements will be broken. Whatever options a group decides upon, it seems best if decisions on how to ensure accountability are as inclusive, and localised as possible. In this way, if a community were to decide they wanted a system of sanctions, then at least if they used it, whoever was being punished would have been been part of setting that system up in the first place. For example, many co-operatives today work together to create a grievance and disciplinary procedure, which usually involves outlining unwanted behaviours (including 'not abiding by co-op decisions') and setting up a system of warnings which lead up to exclusion. Of course, exclusion in itself is more appropriate in some cases than others. For example, if someone is repeatedly violent and you think they are likely to continue, then exclusion is equivalent to saying, "Go and beat up someone else." However, the idea of a pre-agreed process and set of consequences could be used with a range of different outcomes. Communities with a less formal approach might use a more case by case process of working out with everyone involved how to deal with a situation in a way that enabled everyone's safety.

Involvement and efficiency

The section above presents a pragmatic case for everyone being as involved as possible in decision making: if everyone is equally involved, they will have more of a stake in things, and are more likely to stick to what is agreed, making the system much more stable. The model of decision making we describe maximises inclusion by placing the responsibility for most decision making at the most local level possible. However, even within this model, there is potential for one individual or group to accumulate power, and potentially use it to uphold their own interests against others. The things that we do to limit this accumulation of power can be time-consuming, sometimes debilitatingly so. What can we do to strike the right balance?

For example, imagine a street in which only one person knows about the shared finances, one person is always the delegate to spokescouncils, and just one person has any skills in electrics. It would be very easy for the finances person to say that an idea they didn't like was too expensive, and no-one would be able to contradict them. This might be about them not being totally honest with themselves, rather than about any conscious manipulation, but either way the effects could be the same. The delegate to spokescouncils might have even more potential to pick up undue influence on decisions. How often have you come out of a meeting and discovered that everyone had slightly (or vastly) different ideas about what had been agreed? Consider the possibilities of distorted communication within the group and in reporting to and from the spokescouncil. Theoretically, the electrician has less power over others – they could make practical decisions like where the wires should go, and the group as a whole could make the decisions about what the end result should be like, for example whether every building needs connecting up to the solar array. However, this too requires trust, and trustworthiness. When the electrician says that a particular plan is 'impossible' how is everyone to know whether they actually mean 'a lot of work for me', for example?

There are things people in this street could do to make things more equal. Roles could be shared and rotated. Clear records of decisions could be taken so that the spoke's mandate is clear. Whoever takes on a particular role could feedback regularly, or keep thorough and accessible records. Necessary information can be prepared in advance of meetings so that everyone can meaningfully input. However, this all takes time. Time to skill-share when tasks are rotated. Time to work out how to express your specialised knowledge in a way that is detailed enough, but also clear and simple for people who don't have the same expertise in the area. Time to prepare meetings so that everyone can participate in them. Time to record decisions so that you all understand the same thing at the time, as well being able to check that they are being implemented, and tell people who weren't there.

The time question can be put into perspective. For example, most people who have been involved in lengthy meetings today are likely to have experienced some frustrations(!) However, consider one of those frustrating meetings and compare the necessary time spent making decisions to the time spent going off on tangents or quibbling over minor details because no-one dared name the real source of a conflict or floundering about because you don't have enough information to make a decision. In other words, you might find that a lot of the frustration came from trying to do collective decision making in a culture that often doesn't have the skills, rather than its being intrinsic to meetings.

Another way to put the time question into perspective is to think about all the time we lose in the current system. Many people spend a large proportion of their waking hours going to work to earn money. Some of that time will never be recompensed in wages – it will simply provide profit to their employer. A massive chunk of the money they do get will be spent on their home – not just on essential repairs, but providing more profit for a mortgage provider or landlord because they have a piece of paper saying they are entitled to collect money in return for you living in a building that is just standing there. Then there is the time we spend earning money that goes on tax. This money is not entirely 'lost' to us – as a society we get it back every time someone has their recycling taken away or gets treated for cancer or borrows a book from the library. However, in the current system we hand over almost complete control of where that money goes. In this way, some of the hours we put in at work enable the state to afford not just hospitals and schools, but also nuclear weapons and the financial clout to come off on top in international negotiations. This compulsory appropriation of our time through various channels is so normalised that most of the time we're not even aware of it. But in a society in which we made our decisions as free and equal people, it seems unlikely that anyone would voluntarily give away hours of their time for someone else's profit, like we do when we work for a private company or pay to live somewhere. We would be much more likely to give the equivalent of tax – offering material things (like time, money or other units of exchange) to communal services. However, when we are part of making decisions about how such services are run then it is likely to feel less like such things are simply taken away from us. Therefore, (unless we are very bad at our meetings!) the time that it takes to make decision making inclusive could be compensated by getting back the time which is invisibly given away in the current system.

However, even in the most efficient group in the world there will still be a tension between the desire for everyone affected to get fully involved, and the need or desire to spend time doing other things. Every group can work out which areas are particularly important to prioritise involvement in and which it is more acceptable to allow short cuts to be taken for. Looking at the examples above, the group might be totally happy to trust the expertise of the electrician without asking questions, but they might want the finances to be done by one person for a maximum of five years with thorough records accessible to all, and their spokespeople to rotate every six months with thorough consultation on each decision.

What about the people who don't want to be involved?

There are always likely to be people who don't want to come to meetings. This could be for a variety of reasons, not just lack of engagement, but, for example, meeting burn-out, general stress or illness, even a trust that other members of the collective will reach the 'right' decision. Such people obviously shouldn't be forced to take part, but similarly, they may have to live with the consequences of any decision they decided not to participate in. When faced with non-participating members collectives should at least make the effort to make sure that everyone who may be affected is aware of the decisions that are being taken. The reasons for non-participation should be worked out, and ways of encouraging and enabling participation should be considered.

So what do we do with all these unanswered questions?

The ideas that we offer clearly do not provide a simple home over the rainbow where all of humanity's problems will be sorted out. *Some* of the suggestions we have made involve uniting different ideals. For example, it is possible for decision making to become more inclusive *and* quicker with the use of good facilitation in your meetings. It is possible for someone to experience freedom without exerting power over someone else if both people can be involved in looking for a decision that truly works for everyone. But sometimes all we can do is look for the best balance between different imperfect options. In the examples above, however good your facilitation, it will still take more time getting everyone fully involved in discussion than using short cuts like considering one pre-formed proposal. So a community will have to make case by case decisions about whether to prioritise speed or inclusion in a given circumstance. If you can't find a solution which genuinely works for everyone involved, then some people will feel they are losing some personal freedom to the group. A community whose guiding principles are freedom and equality will have to find its own answers to these problems by trying things out and reflecting on how that is working, then trying more things out until they reach a system that they can live with.

If you find the lack of perfect answers discouraging, it is important to remember that the current system doesn't come anywhere near to getting any of these things right. If your life is relatively free and comfortable then, globally speaking, you are enjoying a rare privilege. This doesn't mean you don't have the *right* to be free and comfortable, but that your comfort is not an indication that everyone else is OK too. For example, a financially well-to-do person living in Britain may be intellectually aware of the injustice and exploitation involved in things like sweat shop labour, corporate land grabbing and the extinction of other species, but not feel the same daily emotional pressure they would if they were living these things first hand. We don't say this to trigger your guilt responses: none of us chose the world we were born into. But, we can choose to see it for what it is, and work for something better.

How do we get there?

So, as an individual, or a group, or even a 'social justice movement', what can we do now that brings us any closer to realising the potential for another, fairer world?

Thinking about these questions as an individual or a group, it is clear that anything you choose to do will only be a small part of the overall picture. You cannot wake up one morning and say 'I am going to transform society today.' However, this does not necessarily mean that you might as well stay in bed waiting for someone else to do it. There are a number of different ideas about what are the best things to do in the present to support the possibility of real change that gets to the root of the problem. Without a crystal ball, it is hard to know which will have the best outcomes. We have presented a few of the ideas that are already out there. This is neither a comprehensive list nor a coherent strategy – the aim is to spark your thinking processes about what fits your priorities, skills and situation.

The scale of change we are taking about cannot be achieved by booting out individual politicians or business leaders, but only by removing the structures which give them power. This kind of total shake-up of society is often described as 'the' revolution. However, getting rid of today's power structures is only part of the story. An uprising may be spontaneous, but an organised society like the one we describe is unlikely to organically 'emerge' from the ruins of state capitalism. When we don't have corporations and governments and armies, what happens next? If a successful revolution is followed by chaos, then people are very vulnerable to a new dictator wading in to 'rescue' them, and we could be left with a regime that is more authoritarian than the one we had before. Whatever we put in place is unlikely to survive unless it can set up ways of organising that meet people's basic needs both immediately and in the long term. Therefore, whatever we do needs to keep in mind these two goals, getting rid of the old system, and being able to build something better in its place.

Traditional Models of how change might happen

There are a number of models for how the current system might end and a new one be put in its place. Broadly speaking they fall into either a Marxist-Leninist or an anarchist/libertarian category. (*NB these categories are very loose, and the systems we are talking about go under many names: the point we are trying to make is that there are a variety of ideas out there.*)

Marxism-Leninism

The basic theory is that capitalism will create a society so divided and unequal that exploited workers will start a revolution. There will then be a transition period (socialism) in which a worker-controlled dictatorship will oversee the development of a new, more egalitarian society. Once a culture has developed that takes co-operation and equality as the norm, then the dictatorship will be able to wither away, leaving a communist society to manage itself based on these principles. History provides plenty of examples of societies that have entered the first stages, of a revolution followed by a dictatorship: the Soviet Union, China etc. However, what these examples suggest is that power, once gained, is very hard to give up, and new systems may end up exerting at least as much control over people's lives than what they replaced.[1]

---

[1] On the other hand, genuine attempts to devolve power in Marxist-Leninist inspired political systems have led at best to a shift to whatever the current international default system of control is (e.g. Hungarian Republic reforms in 1988-89, leading to the introduction of Western-style liberal capitalism), or otherwise to brutal repression, such as the 'Prague Spring' of the Czechoslovakian Socialist Republic: in 1968 the Communist Party started a process of democratisation, decentralisation and greater freedom for the population (such as ending both censorship of the press and surveillance by secret police). This was quickly suppressed by an invasion by allied Marxist-Leninist states.

Anarchist/Libertarian[2]

In terms of making decisions by consensus and of co-operating with other people and groups we feel there are many useful ideas in the history and philosophies of anarchism. Although there are many respected thinkers in the history of anarchy, none have (or presumably ever wanted) the ideological status accorded to Marx, Lenin, Trotsky, Stalin, Mao etc. Consequently there are much more than a handful of ideas of how we get from here to our utopian society. We've taken the liberty (again!) of oversimplifying into two main categories: 're-volution/crisis'; and 'building a new society in the shell of the existing one'.

The basic idea of a **revolution** is that the people who have been down-trodden and exploited by the current system come together to overthrow it. This could be the spontaneous response to a major crisis, or the result of years of political organising.

Another strand of thought involves **evolution** or **building our new society in the shell of the old.** This relies on creating and developing 'parallel' systems. These are alternatives that exist alongside (and within) a capitalist economy, but provide more egalitarian ways of meeting our needs, for example through community groups, grassroots co-operatives and alternative economies.

Some people hold a strong preference for one or other of these strategies. Some believe parallel structures could keep expanding until they replace current systems so that a new system evolves without any need for dramatic upheaval. Others place all their emphasis on revolution, and critique parallel structures because these currently only provide alternatives for a small subset of society, and often make compromises to survive in a capitalist system. However, for many people, revolution and the building of parallel structures are complementary strategies. As we have said, while insurrection or internal collapse may be needed to get rid of the existing system, and this may even happen spontaneously, (like a popular uprising following a sudden economic crisis), the more building blocks that have already been laid, the more easily created a new system can be. Parallel institutions (like co-ops), as well as more explicitly political

---

[2] We use the word Libertarian in its old-fashioned sense, implying desire for liberty in all areas of life, rather than the free-market capitalism sense of the word that has become widespread, particularly in North America.

groups set up to confront power can provide these building blocks – they develop the ideas, skills and connections necessary for self-organising and large scale co-operation.

Whether or not you have a preference for either of these strategies (or some totally different ideas!) we have assumed that most readers of this book will be working towards a society that is brought about voluntarily by people who will live in it (rather than the Marxist idea of an equal society being initially imposed by a dictatorship, and freedom coming later, if and when society as a whole is 'ready' to live voluntarily as equals).

Tactics for the present

We don't attempt to sketch a complete map from here to a political utopia. The context in which major change happens will undoubtedly throw up challenges which we do not specifically address here, like how to to survive ecological collapse or violent suppression by a would-be dictator. When faced with a tank or a tidal wave, consensus probably won't be the first tool in the box! What we can offer are thoughts on what might be a first few steps in the direction of the society we'd like to see, starting from the present.

So, assuming the overall idea is to bring about a new society through some kind of combination of revolution and building a new society in the shell of the old, what tactics can we use now to bring us any closer to our goals? Creating a new society can be done gradually and piecemeal; a revolution is something that happens over a short period in the right historical moment. This doesn't mean we should sit back and wait for it: there are things we can do that might help us to create and seize that historical moment if it arrives. Many of these things can also help us to build a new society, for example, what we do to foment rebellion can also involve modelling and developing more democratic ways of organising. Therefore, we have divided possible tactics up into three broad, overlapping categories which all work to a certain extent within both strategies: confronting power, building alternatives and culture change. We offer a few thoughts about how each might be done well to give us the best chances in an uncertain future.

Case study: Redistribution of resources

After a demonstration in Budapest was gunned down by secret police in 1956 a general strike broke out throught much of Hungary. The government collapsed, and over 2000 workers' and peasants' councils were set up in workplaces, villages and towns. The 'New Hungarian National Government' was declared by moderates, but was largely sidelined or ignored as land was redistributed to those who could work it, and food was taken to the towns to feed the urban population.

The revolution was crushed by Soviet tanks after just over two weeks, but the Hungarian Revolution is remarkable for the speed in which resources such as land and the means of production were locally redistributed to those involved in maintaining and using them.

Confronting power

On one level, those with power over us have it because they have the wealth or force to punish and reward us – we do what they say either because they pay us to do it, or because they have police and armies to make us do it. However, another way of looking at the relationship is that those with power have it because *we* give it to them, for as long as we do what they want us to. As soon as we stop complying, or actually prevent them doing what *they* want, they lose that power. From challenging a sexist comment to organising a strike to smashing up a fighter plane, confronting injustice can have a small, destabilising impact on 'the system'. This is not to claim that any slight act of resistance is a direct stepping stone to revolution. Nor is it to glamorise all rebellion for its own sake. There are things we can do which have a much greater impact than others, and there are things which have disproportionate consequences for ourselves. Unless we want a movement of heroic martyrs, the question is how to use confrontation strategically, to have the maximum destabilising effect, whilst retaining our own strength and resilience.

A crucial question is the support we give each other – in what form that is needed depends on what you plan to do. The labour strike is the classic example of activism that is much more effective with the engagement of everyone affected – the workforce and anyone who might be tempted into working in their place. A handful of people could smash up a fighter plane, but these individuals will rely upon others to sustain them through court cases or whatever else the aftermath might involve. Even something as simple as challenging a sexist comment can be a much more empowering experience when you know that other people will back you up. This doesn't mean that a small number of people can't achieve anything – rather that it helps to think carefully about the extent you will rely on the support of others, and work out how you can ask for that, or do things where you are less reliant on numbers.

Another question is where to target confrontational activism. Some people like protests at world summits or one-off actions against hubs of gross concentrated power like banks or power stations because this allows them to pit themselves against capitalism, climate change or 'the system' in general. Actions like these provide a springboard for opening up debate, or raising awareness about how the world is run and the alternatives that are possible. For others a coherent campaign against a more specific target holds greater chance of immediate impact. The scale of change may be small: addressing the exploitative work practices of one minor company, or stopping a new supermarket opening in a small town, for example. However, creating measurable change of any kind can be more empowering and inspiring for some than the kind of diffuse impact we have when we take on bigger targets.

Building alternatives

By building more aware, co-operative and consensus based pockets of society now we can prepare for an uncertain future. In part, that is about building structures that can start to take over some of the functions of today's economy and political system and demonstrate that there are other ways of working. It can also be about having some organisations in place that can be scaled up or replicated if capitalist and state institutions implode, or get torn down. For example, if the national currency collapses, we could use alternative economies such as time banks, local exchange trading systems, and barter networks. The transition may be easier if these systems exist and are used already – there will be some people with the skills and ideas, and some infrastructure in place that could be used. For example, a time bank that was administered through a website could easily expand to encompass a lot more people and their skills. In other situations replication of existing organisations might be a better plan: a village food co-op selling vegetables from local farms might suddenly be inundated if the supermarket supply chain failed. Possible options could be to take over more space, and buy up a bigger proportion of the local produce. However the supply of food could possibly be spread out more effectively if one member of staff devoted their time to visiting other villages and helping them set up

Case study: Alternative currencies

In central Europe in the 1920s and 30s local currencies ensured employment and affordable food and accommodation, despite hyperinflation in national currencies. For example, the local council in Wörgl (Austria) issued 32,000 Schillings in Freigeld in 1932. Freigeld is a local, convertible currency which loses value over time. In the case of Wörgl the money lost 1% of its value every month, which ensured that it was spent quickly – circulation was estimated at 400 times over 14 months. This allowed the council to spend on civic regeneration, creating jobs and taking the local area out of recession: unemployment (rising dramatically in the rest of the country) fell from 21% to 15% over 14 months. By 1933 other councils began to express an interest in issuing their own Freigeld, and the state threatened to send in the army if Wörgl council did not withdraw its local currency.

their own food co-ops. In many cases, expansion or replication won't be an either/or choice – existing units will be able to expand a little before splitting up to prevent decision making and accountability becoming unwieldy and to allow people to do things in the ways that suit them. Either way, the better the systems an organisation develops now, the better placed they will be to welcome new people or pass on their model to others at a point where it is needed.

Culture change

We first introduced these categories as 'overlapping'. Broadly speaking, what we do to confront power and create alternatives is worth it for the immediate effects it has – rescuing one fox from the hunt, changing a discriminatory education admissions policy or creating a way for some people to use other people's unwanted stuff. However, these activities can also be a means of creating the possibilities of a culture that is more co-operative, more empowered and more equal. This doesn't mean setting out to manipulate people into changing their culture – it means creating space for different kinds of behaviour and interaction to grow, and letting people decide for themselves what works for them.

Where we're at now

What kind of culture change needs to happen will depend on the culture from which you are reading this. As Seeds for Change, we write in capitalist northern-western Europe, and this is the only context we feel qualified to talk about. We observe a number of elements of that culture that prop up the current system, and make the creation of a new one more challenging.

One of the most obvious examples is the way we are encouraged to **compete and conform** for survival within the system – while each individual is trying to make sure they are the one to get a council house or university place or job, then we are not getting together to address the underlying problem of there not being enough to go round, and the overall effect is to increase inequality. While we buy into the idea that we need to be the same as other people to be accepted we aren't making space for the real acceptance we experience when people take us as we actually are. This mentality can leak into our decision making – the desire to conform making us less open and trusting, the habit of competition reinforcing hierarchies and making us less able to work together as empowered equals.

Along with competitiveness and conformity goes **atomisation**. In countries like Britain today, many people don't even know their neighbours. Their social lives usually involve a closed circle of friends and some people they work or study with. Outside these closed circles they spend their day weaving in and out of strangers, perhaps a quick nod to a familiar face, a few ritual conversations at the bus stop, and an exchange of minor favours, like feeding next door's cat. This clearly poses a challenge for a decision-making model which relies upon a unit like the street being the place where the fundamentals of daily life get worked out, and upon humans being able to co-operate across wide geographical areas.

As well as the attitudes, our society often lacks the **skills** that go along with a more communal way of life. Hierarchical systems prepare us to do what we're told, or to tell others what to do, but not to *share* responsibility – even something as simple as organising a holiday between a group of friends can founder because people are not in the habit of facilitating group conversations about things like what everyone can afford or even where to go. This can make meetings about minor uncontroversial topics a frustrating experience, never mind negotiating through conflict under pressure. If society dramatically changed, we can expect that people would pick up new skills, possibly very quickly. However, developing confidence through long term positive experience can help us keep problem-solving when things didn't work first time.

Finally there is a question of **political analysis and vision**. Dissatisfaction with politicians and cynicism about advertising is widespread. However, there often seems to be a lack of follow-through – people continue to vote for the same parties and buy the same products, in spite of an uneasy awareness that neither will quite do what it says on the tin. It is not clear to what extent this is about not being convinced by or aware of alternatives, or to what extent it's about a reasonable desire to get on with the life that is familiar, rather than invest time and energy in the uncertainty of change. Either way, if we are looking for a free and equal society then people can't be forced, persuaded or deceived into going along with it. They might rally round an attractive idea in a moment of crisis but if this is the first time they have thought about politics then leaders can offer more enticing quick fixes ("Vote for me and I'll make things fair.") It is understandable that many people crave safety and stability, and even a dictator who offers this at a time of unrest, (along with special benefits for their supporters) is likely to get some kind of a following. If a society is to be co-owned from the bottom up, then the people who will live in it need to be actively involved in creating visions for how it might look, and have a realistic idea about what that entails, not to mention a healthy cynicism about the promises of anyone who offers easier options.

Case study: Culture change

After the German armed forces in Berlin surrendered to the Red Army in May 1945 there was a period of several weeks before arrangements were made to provide for the civilian population, and to start rebuilding the city. Nevertheless, the day after the surrender, workers at a cable factory in southeast Berlin picked their way through the ruined city to what was left of their workplace. The bosses and the Nazi commissars had fled, or were in hiding, but the workers started to salvage what they could of the machinery, soon managing to begin production again. Other workers from the plant went out into the surrounding countryside to find food and fuel to share out back at the factory.

This was by no means unique in Berlin or the rest of Europe at this time but the desire of these and other workers to begin organising their workplace themselves, and to take care of each other, is notable when placed in the context of the period. In 1945 they had endured (or even participated in) 12 years of Nazi rule, a time of suspicion, fear and ceaseless propaganda demonising 'the weak' in society, and condemning co-operation and solidarity.

We find this example inspiring because it shows how humans have the capacity to look after and consider each other's needs despite being subject to extremely negative and pervasive socialisation.

A Consensus Handbook

What can be done?

So what do we do with this mismatch? To a certain extent we can place some hope in examples of how people have pulled together and started self-organising when there has been a sudden vacuum of power – culture can change very rapidly when the situation in which we live also changes (see box on previous page). However, we can increase our chances of success if do what we can to build the equal, honest relationships, the skills and the political awareness that a healthier society can grow from. The suggestions we make here just scratch the surface of the possibilities out there. Likewise, they only scratch the surface of the changes that would need to be made! However, we need to start somewhere, so here are a few ideas on how things might be done.

Share ideas

We have said that a new society relies upon real involvement from a wide range of people. To create a society that is truly free and equal this needs to be the voluntary involvement of people who go in with their eyes open, not recruits and converts who've been drafted in by the hard sell. Of course, we may want to counter the powerful propaganda machine of state capitalism – we don't need to hold back from giving people *access* to alternative possibilities and ways of looking at the world. But if we rely on rosy promises or set out to *persuade* people then we assume they cannot make intelligent choices about what to believe – an assumption that runs counter to the very society we are trying to create. Being open about politics without ramming it down people's throats is a delicate art as well as an important one. Starting where people are currently at is a pretty important principle – for example, leaping straight in with a fully developed model for utopia when someone comments on the unreliability of their MP may be a bit too much! For thoughts on how to share ideas, see Chapter 8: *Bridging the gap*, page 170.

Creating settings in which people can experience different ways of organising can fulfil a similar function of passing on new ideas, but leave people space to think for themselves about how well they work. Even if we just organise events or particular projects that give only short or marginal opportunities for involvement (whether that's a protest camp or a community group meeting once a month), the exposure we can provide to respectful communication and decision making can give people a sense of what is possible, an awareness that our society can be organised differently. We have seen many times that even just a single experience of a well facilitated consensus meeting has inspired people to think critically about the status quo, and how things can be changed. However, that critical thought also needs somewhere to go – longer term projects that are embedded in a community, and provide a viable way for people to meet their needs have a greater influence on how people see the world as well as having a more real material impact.

Model alternative ways of working and make them accessible

Having a wide range of different types of parallel systems will help more people access co-operative organising skills. For example, something like a freecycle network, a mental health service-users' self-help group or an allotment association may include people who don't see themselves as 'political' in any way. For others, anger is a great mobilising force – they will start engaging in campaign groups when they are threatened by something external, like a new road being built through their village, or welfare benefits being taken away. These alternatives don't even have to be groups as such – you can build connections within your community more informally by organising a street party, or knocking on doors in your tower block and trying to come up with a collective response when the landlord repeatedly fails to fix the stair lights. If this is too much then even inviting the neighbours round for a cup of tea could be a start!

Accessibility is about more than *what* you are doing – see Chapter 8: *Bridging the gap* for some steps your group can take to avoid replicating the exclusion and oppression that characterises mainstream society.

Develop skills

As usual, it is worth thinking about *how* we do these things – if we have meetings where we are stressed, anxious and bossy the co-operative skills we gain and pass on may be minimal. If our activism is ineffective and badly thought through then what we do may be less than inspirational. Remember, we don't necessarily *achieve* more by frantically *doing* more. Looking after ourselves and each other and taking the care and time to do things well is likely to be more effective in the long run.

The section *Challenges, questions and tensions* above outlined some of the difficulties we might face, trying to organise society along libertarian and egalitarian lines. We didn't offer perfect, one-size-fits-all solutions, but suggested that groups could find their own practical techniques to make things work. This work doesn't need to wait til a new society forms. We grapple with these kinds of questions whenever we try to work non-hierarchically. For example, a network of groups running a campaign will face some of these questions, like how to respond when some of the local groups don't stick to decisions that were made collectively. Smaller, more close knit collectives, like a workers' co-op or an affinity group which regularly does actions together may only include a few people at a time. However, the experience of working together over a long period can create the commitment and will to develop some of the more 'involved' skills that this book covers, like tackling power dynamics, or collaborating to find a way out of conflict.

Share skills

Developing skills only becomes useful to society as a whole when we are able to pass them on. In activism it is common for cliques to form, of people who share political ideology, culture and lifestyle. They can develop their own jargon and sometimes a whole language of 'hand signals'. This easy, comfortable communication may help

with their specific aims, like setting up a housing co-op, or doing direct action together. However, if they remain socially isolated and don't take the time to build up trust, openness and good communication with a wider community, it is unlikely that they will be able to effectively share their co-operative organising skills in a moment of crisis. Instead, their confidence and experience may put them into the role of unofficial leaders, or mean that they are resented and not listened to at all. Similarly, if they have spent their politically active life only associating with people who use the same language to express the same opinions, they may be less able to listen to and respect the very different views and needs of their neighbours.

Sharing skills therefore is not just about running workshops. This can be a great idea for people who already want to know more about something (see Appendix: *Short guide to facilitating workshops*). However, it is also important to think about how to make your skills accessible to wider range of people. As always, there is a tricky balance to be struck so that you offer your skills in a way that enables and empowers other people, rather than taking over the role so that no-one feels able step into it.

Create a more equal society in the here and now

The more we can do now to unpick the inequalities between us, the better placed we will be to make decisions as empowered equals in a consensus based society. Chapter 8: *Bridging the gap* looks at approaches you can take to sorting out power dynamics in consensus groups. Outside these groups, though there are, in most cases, wider inequalities to be tackled. On a day to day level, the status quo can be eroded when individuals take opportunities to challenge the behaviour and assumptions of people in their wider community. For a more concentrated impact, it can help to get together with other people affected by the same form of oppression, and form groups dedicated to tackling it, as well as to empowering yourselves. If these groups connect and co-ordinate with each other, and potentially draw on support from outside people and groups, then a broader movement can be formed that works against all oppression, not just that which is targeted at particular identities.

A Consensus Handbook

A final thought

When you look at the scale of change that is needed then anything you choose to do can feel like chipping away at a mountain face with a toothpick, or emptying an ocean with a thimble. As well as scale, there is the question of compromise: something is lost in translation between your elegant visions of the future and the day to day reality of getting on with your colleagues or writing leaflets for your campaign. However, try turning this on its head. If we really believe in freedom and equality, and shared power, then how could anyone think that a better world for 9 billion people could be delivered by one person single-handedly? Unless we intend to set up a dictatorship that stamps our vision across the entire globe, then we will have to accept that the impacts of what we do will be diffuse, localised or both. In other words, if we aren't trying to set up a society that gives a huge amount of power to any individual, then it follows that the process of getting there will also involve thousands upon millions of people and groups all doing their thing and co-ordinating as best they can. If you happen to live through a period of intense revolutionary activity, you will have been enabled to do this by all the generations that went before you. And if you never see significant change in your lifetime, your step-kid's children's neighbour's nieces who do will still owe a small part of 'their' achievements to your efforts today. And in the meantime, the small material difference we make when we set up a co-op or organise an empowering community meeting or save a small belt of woodland is worth it because real life is in the here and now.

Afterword

The way we make decisions is an important part of how we put our political or ethical beliefs into practice. Consensus is based on principles of freedom and equality – it aims to find a balance between the needs of the individual to have control over what they sign up to, and the needs of the group to work together in order to gets things done. It rejects the idea that for one person to win, someone else has to lose; instead we think creatively to find solutions that the whole group can be happy with. Even when there is no such perfect solution to be found, the process re-affirms our commitment to each other, making it much more possible to willingly accept compromise for the sake of the group.

However, reaching decisions that have the true, meaningful consent of everyone involved can be tricky at the best of times. And usually there are some extra complications to deal with – being a very large group, or all living in different parts of the world, or having simmering conflicts that have never been addressed. Dealing with these situations well can take dedication, positivity and patience, and when our own energy is not matched by other people's we can easily get frustrated.

At the same time, when consensus achieves what it sets out to do in a difficult situation it puts our other experiences of decision making into a new perspective. We realise that it isn't necessary to give up our own freedom in order to work with others. We do not need to hand over our power to a few remote politicians or union leaders or employers, we do not need to try to win. We can be trusting and open and expect honesty and consideration in return.

When we struggle with shared responsibility, then in large part this may be because we aren't used to it, not because it is intrinsically more difficult than other ways of making decisions. It requires us to learn some skills and knowledge we haven't grown up with, but with practice and will, we can learn. For example, we work out how a large group meeting could be structured to allow everyone to be included, how to make any meeting more effective and enjoyable, and how to deal with power imbalances or a conflict head-on without losing respect for the other people involved in those unhealthy dynamics.

Learning these things is about more than making our own particular group work better. It is about developing the skills as a society that could open the door to new ways of working together – based on collective control and direct democracy. We believe that the skills, attitudes and conditions that underpin consensus decision making are what we need – whether in a small group or in the whole world – to live together on a basis of freedom, equality and shared power.

Appendix: Short guide to facilitating workshops

So you've been asked to run a workshop or skillshare?

Sharing knowledge and skills is an important part of contributing to our communities – and doing this means the wheel doesn't have to be continually reinvented. Perhaps more importantly, when we pass on skills to others, it is less likely that informal hierarchies will build up in our groups. In this guide we go through the basic steps that can help your workshop really work for you and your group.

Preparation

Preparation is the key to a good workshop, and it also helps you to be more confident. An **agenda,** or **workshop plan,** is a good way to make sure you're adequately prepared, and that you are being sensible about what you can cover in the time you have. It's always tempting to try to cram in too much, so be realistic about how much time you give to activities, and be brutal about taking stuff out!

First of all work out your aims for the workshop – you may find it helps to write them out at the top of the agenda when you're working on it. Come back to these as you plan each activity. Does what you are planning to do help you achieve your workshop aims, or help the group relax and get to know each other? If not, you probably don't need the activity.

How to design your workshop

We're used to workshops that end up being presentations or group discussions. They're easier to organise, but with just a little bit of work we can help participants learn much more from our workshops – and enjoy them more too! People remember better if they are actively involved in their own learning, and if the workshop is interesting and dynamic.

Teacher or lecturer	Facilitator

Teacher is an 'expert'. Learning from few to many. Learners have less control of their learning.	Only expertise needed is facilitation. Knowledge drawn from the group and shared. Learners can set the agenda and share skills and knowledge

Facilitating a workshop is about helping your group to share their own experiences. You can also add your own experiences and knowledge, but the key is that everyone is really involved.

Ask yourself whether someone in the group might already know or have some experience in your topic. If you think they might have, work out a way to get them to contribute – you could use an ideastorm or split your participants up into smaller groups and give them a task. Even if the knowledge comes mostly from you, you can plan games, role plays or practice sessions and chances for participants to reflect on their experiences to make your workshop more participatory.

> ## The agenda mix
> We all learn in different ways so the best thing to do is to in-clude different kinds of exercises and tools in your workshop. If you can get your participants listening, thinking, moving around and contributing at different points during your work-shop the chances are that everyone will enjoy it!
>
> It's a good idea to make sure that people move around every 90 minutes or so – a quick <u>energiser</u>, physical activity or just changing seats can help stop people nodding off!
>
> Have a look at Chapter 6: *Facilitation techniques and activities* to get some ideas of how to vary your workshop.

Practical exercises

If your workshop is about practical things (like how to do a news re-lease or wire up a solar panel) then make sure to add enough time for people to try out their new skills. This helps build people's con-fidence and means they're more likely to remember what they've learnt, especially if they get the chance to try things out several times, not just the once.

Breaks

When designing a workshop it's easy to forget the breaks – there al-ways seems to be more to fit in than time will allow! But we're all human, both facilitators and participants, and when we're tired we don't function too well – and that includes understanding and re-membering what the workshop was about.

If your workshop is two hours or less it's usually enough to make sure there is a possibility to get tea or coffee (or a trip to the pub) at the end. But if your workshop is longer than two hours then it's a good idea to schedule in a break every 90 minutes or so, with an en-ergiser in between.

A Consensus Handbook

Preparation checklist

★ Have you included a good balance of different types of activities?

★ Have you made time for practical sessions, breaks and energisers?

★ Have you thought through what you're going to say and how you're going to do things?

★ Are all the practicalities like publicity, venue, seating, refreshments etc. sorted?

★ Do you have all the materials you need?

★ Have you checked whether anyone has particular needs, and how you can cater for those?

Want to find out more?

This short guide introduces some of the things you can do to make your workshop enjoyable and productive. If you want to find out more about facilitating workshops and the tools you can use have a look at the longer briefings on our website.

Glossary

Some of the words in this glossary have a specific meaning in the context of consensus, and this is the definition we have listed.

Action point: A task that needs to be completed. For example, a meeting might produce a list of action points with people assigned to them and deadlines for completion.

Active listening: The act of suspending your own thoughts and truly listening to what somebody is saying in an attempt to understand them better.

Affinity group: A small group of people who plan and take action together; sometimes as a one off but often long-term.

Agenda: A list of things to be talked about in a meeting.

Amendment: An amendment enhances a proposal. It's not a new idea, but a way of making an existing one more effective.

Atomisation: A society that is separated into individual units, for example households, with very little connection or communication between them.

Block: An option when testing for agreement in consensus. If you block you are saying: "There is a fundamental problem with the core of this proposal that cannot be resolved, we need to look for a new proposal."

Closed group: A group where membership is restricted. For example, new people can't join at all, or only with the agreement of all other members, or only if they fit certain criteria. For example, a workers' co-op might only be open to people who are suitable for employment in that particular kind of work.

Co-operative, co-op: A democratic group owned by the members. This might be workers (a workers' co-op), people who live there (a housing co-op), people who shop there (a consumer co-op) etc.

Consensus: Consensus is a way of making decisions in a group where everyone involved must consent to the final outcome.

Consensus-minus-one: A way of making decisions in a group where the consent of everyone is sought. If just one person withholds that consent, the decision can go ahead, but if any more do then a new proposal must be found.

Delegate (noun): A person who takes responsibility for representing their group's views at other meetings, especially spokescouncils (see *Spokescouncil*).

Delegate (verb): To pass on responsibility for something.

Facilitation: Generally speaking, any activity that makes a task easier for others. In this context we are talking about making meetings more effective and inclusive.

Facilitator: Someone who takes responsibility for the facilitation of a meeting (see *Facilitation*).

A Consensus Handbook

Federal: This describes a political system based on independent small groups co-ordinating via a wider network on decisions which affect them all.

Informal hierarchy: When a group appears to operate on a basis of equality (for example, they make decisions by consensus, and no-one officially has any more power than anyone else) but in practice some people have greater influence and status than others.

Majority vote: A way of making decisions in which something can go ahead if more than 50% of the people involved agrees to it (see *Super-majority vote*).

Micro-management: a) Somebody dictating or checking every little thing someone else does. b) An entire group being involved involved together in every tiny decision and working out the fine detail together.

Minutes: A written record of a meeting. Minutes should be an accurate account of the meeting including the main points of discussion, decisions reached and actions to be taken.

Open group: A group anyone can join.

Plenary: A meeting involving everyone in a group or organisation – this word is often used in the context of very big meetings.

Proposal: A proposal is a suggested final decision, which will then be tested to see if everyone can agree to it. In consensus, a proposal should be based on listening to discussion of the issue, and should be an idea that could be acceptable to everyone.

Ratification: Confirming agreement on a decision that has provisionally been made. For example, a network might make a decision, but require member groups to ratify it before it is confirmed.

Reservations: An option when testing for agreement in consensus. If you declare reservations you are saying: "I'm not totally happy with the proposal, but I'll go along with it."

Spoke, spokesperson: A person who takes responsibility for representing their group's views at other meetings, especially spokescouncils (see *Spokescouncil*).

Spokescouncil: A structure for reaching consensus decisions in large groups. The meeting as a whole splits into small groups. Each small group discusses an issue initially and the thoughts and ideas of those small groups are shared with each other by means of a spokescouncil, which involves spokes (delegates) from each group. Discussion continues to pass between the small groups and the spokescouncil until a decision is reached.

Stand aside: An option when testing for agreement in consensus. If you stand aside you are saying "I can't support this proposal and won't implement it; but I don't want to stop the group from going ahead."

Summarise: To repeat the main points of a discussion in an abbreviated or more succinct way.

Super-majority vote: A way of making decisions in which a significant majority (e.g. 80 or 90%) of a group needs to give their support to a proposal before it can go ahead.

Synthesise: To find and highlight the common ground in what people are saying, and weave this together to form a proposal which should work for everyone.

Tool, facilitation tool: A technique or activity used to help a meeting do what it needs to do, for example a go-round or meeting agenda.

Virtual meeting: Holding a meeting in which not all participants are physically present in the same place. For example, a meeting conducted by phone conference or email.

Index